"I'm so impressed with this book! The truth you'll find here is going to transform your life. *Give Yourself a Break* offers insight into the ways we lack compassion for ourselves, how that impacts us, and how we can speak God's truth and grace into our life. When we truly see ourselves the way God does—with love and compassion—it changes everything! But an even greater benefit of this book is that the more compassion we have for ourselves, the more we have to give away. And in the bigger picture of life, that's what it's all about."

—**Barbara Wilson**, bestselling author of *Free: Finding Freedom and Healing from Your Past*

"We hear it every time we fly: 'If the oxygen masks drop, secure your own mask before helping others.' It feels selfish, but if we don't take care of our own needs first, we've lost our ability to help others. Over the years, Kim Fredrickson has watched people value others while ignoring themselves, depleting their own reserves. In *Give Yourself a Break* she guides us back to healthy self-care as the foundation for impacting others. By helping us value ourselves the way God does, she hands us the oxygen mask. Grab it—it's an excellent guide for the journey."

—**Dr. Mike Bechtle**, speaker, consultant, and author of *People Can't Drive You Crazy If You Don't Give Them the Keys*

"Everyone needs to read this book! Kim clearly describes how to deal with the self-critic inside of us. I spent years in therapy learning the concepts in this book, which is what slowly healed my narcissistic injuries, thus healing my own narcissism. It is only when we learn how to be more loving toward ourselves that we can become more loving in our closest relationships. This then gives us the capacity to fulfill the commandment to love others as we love ourselves."

—**Lisa Charlebois**, LCSW, psychotherapist and author of *You Might Be a Narcissist If . . .*

"It's amazing to me that we are taught our whole lives to be nice to others but rarely are we taught to be nice to ourselves. In *Give Yourself a Break* Kim Fredrickson inspires and instructs us into a deeper and fuller way to be nice to ourselves. Be compassionate to yourself and get this book, and apply these truths to your life. It may just be the best thing you will ever do for yourself."

—**Chuck Wysong**, pastor of Life Community Church

"In this unique book, Kim Fredrickson integrates the powerful practice of self-compassion with Christian faith. *Give Yourself a Break* is filled with practical tools and stories of everyday people who successfully learned to treat themselves with care and compassion rather than self-criticism. This book is a must if you yearn to experience what recent studies have shown—the power of self-compassion to positively transform your life and your relationships."

—**Georgia Shaffer, PA**, licensed psychologist and author of *Avoiding the 12 Relationship Mistakes Women Make*

"Sometimes the most destructive relationship we have is with our own self. We beat ourselves up without mercy and are endlessly critical of our sins, flaws, and failures. *Give Yourself a Break* addresses self-hatred and shame in a fresh way and challenges us with a grace-filled approach to seeing our inadequacies and sins."

—**Leslie Vernick**, licensed counselor, coach, speaker, and author of *The Emotionally Destructive Relationship*

Give Yourself a Break

Turning Your **Inner Critic** into a Compassionate Friend

Kim Fredrickson

Revell

a division of Baker Publishing Group
Grand Rapids, Michigan

© 2015 by Kim Fredrickson, MS, MFT (MFT 22635) Roseville, CA

Published by Revell
a division of Baker Publishing Group
P.O. Box 6287, Grand Rapids, MI 49516-6287
www.revellbooks.com

Printed in the United States of America

Library of Congress Cataloging-in-Publication Data
Fredrickson, Kim.
    Give yourself a break : turning your inner critic into a compassionate friend / Kim Fredrickson.
        pages cm
    Includes bibliographical references.
    ISBN 978-0-8007-2441-2 (pbk.)
    1. Self-esteem—Religious aspects—Christianity. 2. Self-acceptance— Religious aspects—Christianity. 3. Self-talk—Religious aspects—Christianity. I. Title.
    BV4598.24.F74 2015
    248.4—dc23   2015003246

Unless otherwise indicated, Scripture quotations are from the Holy Bible, New International Version®. NIV®. Copyright © 1973, 1978, 1984, 2011 by Biblica, Inc.™ Used by permission of Zondervan. All rights reserved worldwide. www.zondervan.com

Scripture quotations labeled KJV are from the King James Version of the Bible.

The author has used many of the exercises and self-soothing tools in this book in her counseling practice over the last thirty years. She had made every effort to give credit where credit is due.

Stories shared in this book are a composite of the many ways people are affected by not having compassion for themselves. No story is a direct reflection of a particular person.

This publication is intended to provide helpful and informative material on the subjects addressed. The author and publisher shall not be liable for your misuse of this material. The author and publisher do not guarantee that anyone following these techniques, suggestions, tips, ideas, or strategies will become successful. The author and publisher expressly disclaim responsibility for any adverse effects arising from the use or application of the information contained in this book.

Published in association with Books & Such Literary Agency.

15 16 17 18 19 20 21   7 6 5 4 3 2

This book is dedicated to my dear family and friends who have been supportive of my ministry to help others heal and reclaim their lives. I send special thanks to my clients over the last thirty years who have helped me to develop compassion and understanding through life's difficulties and triumphs.

A special dedication goes to my dear friends Joany and Betty, who have walked through life with me for more than twenty years with unending support, compassion, and grace. You will both be forever in my heart.

Contents

7

Acknowledgments

Many thanks to my biblical scholar husband, Dave, who checked my Bible references for accuracy and provided continual support for this book, as well as my dear friends who read this book and gave input and critique: Mary Akey, Lisa Charlebois, Pastor Chuck Wysong, Barbara Wilson, Linda Sommerville, Susan Reynolds, Laurie Kroger, and Sue Starkey. Your insights have enriched this work.

Thanks to my two dear children, who have helped me learn about compassion and how to pass that on as their mom. Much appreciation goes to my mom, dad, and sister, who provided me with compassion and love throughout my life.

Thanks to my dear friends Mary, Holly, Susan, and Gretchen, as well as my wonderful colleagues at Valley Psychological Center, who have provided unending support and encouragement.

Thanks so much to my agent, Wendy Lawton with Books and Such Literary Agency, for all of your encouragement. Thanks also to my editor, Vicki Crumpton, and the whole team at Revell. I so appreciate your belief in me and support of this book. What a privilege it has been to partner with all of you.

Introduction

Why Write This Book?

Over my last thirty years as a marriage and family therapist, I have had many, many clients who were very hard on themselves —not because they wanted to be, but because they didn't know what else to do when they failed, made mistakes, made poor decisions, or couldn't foresee the future.

My heart went out to them because I saw them through such different eyes. I saw good people who were doing their best to deal with life. They sometimes succeeded and sometimes failed—just like all of us. What gets us into trouble aren't our failures, but what we do with them. How we treat ourselves when we have unmet needs and encounter failures determines the course of our relationship with ourselves. Many, but not all, of my clients have had a strong belief in God and known that they were forgiven for their sins. However, even with this head knowledge, they didn't always feel forgiven. Instead they felt like they either had to continue to punish themselves for what they'd done, or make up for it because they had no way to let it go.

And so I moved forward with this book when I couldn't find any resources that approached self-compassion (interacting kindly with yourself with both truth and grace) from a faith perspective. Self-compassion is essential for both handling and recovering from the difficulties of life. Without it, we are vulnerable to the opinions of others, as well as the negative messages from the inner critic most of us carry around inside of us.

My hopes for this book are first, that it provides some understanding of why self-compassion is so hard to extend to ourselves, and second, that it provides hope and practical help in learning to relate to ourselves in healthy and gracious ways.

For some of you, individual reading and practice will be just what you need. For others, working through this with a group of trusted friends will be helpful (see appendix B). And for still others, working through this with a kind and compassionate therapist and/or support group will be what you need.

There are different ways to interact with yourself as you process the material in this book. As you work through it, you may want to get a journal and write down your responses to what you've read as well as your reactions to the compassionate messages and self-soothing exercises. Above all, be kind to yourself as you process this information. Don't be surprised if you have mixed responses. Many of us have not received much compassion in our lives, and while we are thirsty for it we may also have a negative reaction to it. If you are one of the many who have this kind of reaction, use it as a way to validate that this is an area of needed internal growth. Trust that you will benefit from this material, and give yourself the support you need; a therapist or support group can help you process this new way of looking at and interacting with yourself. I have seen many, many men and women grow profoundly in their ability to be compassionate with themselves, and there's no reason you can't too!

I wish you the very best as you process this material either individually or as a group. It is my privilege to facilitate your journey of transforming your inner critic into a compassionate friend. I am also walking this journey as I balance interacting with myself kindly with both grace and truth. Let's start a new path together.

1

Why Self-Compassion
Is So Important

> When Jesus landed and saw a large crowd, he had com-
> passion on them and healed their sick.
>
> Matthew 14:14

Does this verse strike you the way it strikes me? Take a breath and notice Jesus's response. When Jesus looked out at this large group of people, his response was compassion for them. He met their needs by healing their sick. He didn't judge them, lecture them, or ignore their needs. What if we could look upon ourselves with Jesus's kind of compassion? It would be life-changing.

You picked up this book for a reason. Something in you said, *Yes, I'd like to give myself a break. I'd like to learn to develop a compassionate relationship with myself.* I'm so glad—and you don't have to go it alone. I will be with you each step of the way as you learn how to understand yourself better. You will find ways to interact with yourself with grace and truth, discover compassionate ways to care for and soothe yourself, and find compassionate words to speak to yourself.

Let's start by defining *self-compassion*.

What it is: compassion is the feeling of pain one feels when another suffers. It is also caring about someone and wishing they not suffer. Self-compassion is having the same concern for our own pain and welfare. Out of self-compassion flow self-care and protection from harm.

What it is not: self-compassion is not self-pity, where we wallow in the shame of what we have done. It is not self-complacency, where we just accept where we are. Instead, it is the idea that we can be kind to ourselves when we fail and treat ourselves with the caring support we would give another who is struggling.

Self-compassion is a balance of truth (*Yes, I made a mistake*) with grace (*I have worth and value, and I will address this mistake directly*).

Self-compassion is absolutely essential for healthy, balanced living. It provides huge benefits including emotional resiliency, stress reduction, contentment, and healthier relationships. Without it we are vulnerable to the opinions of others and find it difficult to deal with and let go of our mistakes. It is tough enough to go through a difficult situation, especially when we think we had a part in creating it. It is another kind of torture to never be able to let go of self-criticism and blame.

Ben was late turning in his quarterly report. *I can't believe I turned in my report late again. I promised myself I wouldn't get behind again. I know my mom's been sick and the basement flooded. That's no excuse! I'm such a loser. I'll never get it right.* When Ben got home from work that day, his dissatisfaction with himself overflowed onto his family as he snapped at his wife, told his daughter to leave him alone, and holed up in his bedroom.

Imagine what it would be like for Ben if he gave himself a break in this situation.

> I can't believe I did that again. I told myself I wouldn't. Let me breathe and think about it. What is the truth? I didn't put it off; it was really important to me to have those reports turned in on time. What went wrong? Well, Mom was sick, and I had to take her to ER—twice! Then four days later the basement flooded, and it took me a day and a half to clean that up and fix the problem. I wasn't being irresponsible . . . sometimes "life" just happens. Even though this is true, I want to come up with solutions to get these reports in on time even when "life" gets in the way. Next time I will start these reports a week earlier to give myself extra time, and I will let my boss know if they might be late and why. I'm a good guy who cares about my job and family. Considering all I had to handle, I did an amazing job.

If Ben responded to himself in this way, with compassion, it would naturally flow to his family. What a difference this would make! By becoming an understanding friend to himself as well as taking the time to give himself both grace and truth, Ben would be able to come home and interact with his family differently. He'd arrive home less flustered, be able to explain to his family what had happened at work, and share with them his caring way of talking with himself. As Ben learns to respond to himself in this way, he is experiencing a core truth: it's all about the relationship. The relationship he has with himself impacts all the other relationships in his life whether he wants it to or not.

God Is Our Example

God's heart is tender toward us in our suffering, frailties, and mistakes. He is our perfect example of balancing truth and grace. He knows we are but dust and is merciful (Ps. 78:38–39). The Bible is full of examples of his compassion toward us and his tenderness to those who are struggling from harm caused by others or by themselves.

Throughout the Bible, God the Father (Old Testament) and Jesus his Son (New Testament) readily had compassion for people when their hearts were open and receptive toward him. When their hearts were hardened, he applied tough love in the hope of softening their hearts so they would come back to him.

We are to model ourselves after God in the way he relates to us. His way is to be drawn to vulnerability and struggle, to respond with compassion and guidance, and to also correct whatever sins or mistakes we've made with grace and truth.

We are often willing to respond to other people with this balanced kindness, but we rarely think that God's example applies to us in the way we interact with ourselves. His grace and compassion apply to each of us individually and collectively. It is wonderful to invest in yourself as you learn to receive compassion from yourself as well as from God.

Inner Peace and Acceptance

When we have compassion for ourselves, our internal negative dialogue goes away. Many people have an ongoing civil war inside their heads. It pains me to even write the words I know many say to themselves: *You're stupid. You're a loser. You should have known better.*

It makes a huge difference when we can balance our response internally after we either make a mistake or regret something we've done or not done. Give this a try: think about a painful moment you had a part in that still hurts when you think about it. Pause to acknowledge the mistake (truth) and also say something encouraging to yourself (grace), such as:

16

Yes, I wish I'd acted differently. I'm also using this experience for good in order to grow and learn. I can grant myself grace while still doing what is necessary to right this situation. I'm not perfect, and I don't need to be. I am lovable and acceptable even when I make mistakes.

Think what a difference it would make in your life if you responded to yourself in this way. Even now, notice how it feels inside to repeat these words. Let the balance of grace and truth delivered kindly sink in deeply. Breathe it in. Yes, it's true. It is possible to be kind to yourself in this way. We have strengths and wonderful attributes as well as weaknesses. We succeed at times as well as fail. This is part of being human. God knows us in all our positives and negatives and loves us completely. He wants to help us, wherever we are.

We get mixed up about this. We often have difficulty realizing that we are personally designed and created by God and are of great worth and value. At the same time we are imperfect, sinful, and hurtful to others and ourselves. It doesn't have to be either/or. We don't have to turn on ourselves when we see our negatives. We can value ourselves while at the same time commit to doing what is necessary to either repair any damage we caused or move toward growth in a specific area.

Emotional Competency, Resilience, and Balance

When we have compassion toward ourselves, we will be able to tolerate and process our feelings in healthy ways. Studies show that self-compassion increases resilience and self-worth, aids in stress reduction, and helps us recover from painful experiences.[1] These are key elements of emotional competency.

Self-compassion is different from self-esteem. Self-esteem is about assessing yourself in a positive way—often in comparison to others, which can lead to narcissism (feeling special or better than others). Self-compassion, on the other hand, is a gentle way we relate to ourselves when we're struggling—with kindness, caring, empathy, and understanding.

New research links self-compassion with better health choices and behaviors.[2] Researchers found that people who eat better, exercise, and have a balance between work and rest do so out of true care for self. This is in direct contrast to attempting these behaviors out of fear, social pressures, or concerns about being compared to others. Changes that are made out of fear or similar motivators rarely last and are often fueled by anxiety, which makes everything worse.

Bad stuff happens—lots of it. Self-compassion helps build resilience, the internal flexibility to rebound and recover from painful, disappointing, and devastating times. Why is this? Because there is a world of difference between going through a difficult time and beating yourself up over and over again and going through that same difficult time while being compassionate and understanding with yourself.

Sherrie put her head in her hands after receiving more bad news. This last year had been rough. First she lost her job when her company downsized, then she had to move to a smaller and more affordable place, and just now she'd received a call from the doctor telling her that her daughter had been diagnosed with type 1 diabetes.

Her first thought was to blame herself for this string of events somehow . . . even though she knew in her head such an accusation wouldn't be true. In the past she would have put herself down, eaten a quart of ice cream, and watched television to numb out. But today she took a deep breath and decided to be a compassionate friend to herself with this recent news. Sherrie allowed herself to have a good cry, prayed to God for help and wisdom, and then called a good friend to get the support she needed.

Sherrie also decided to talk to herself compassionately about the rough year she'd had and then come up with a plan to handle this recent news.

> This has been a tough year. I've had so much to handle and it seems like the tough times just keep coming. It feels like I can't handle one more thing, but I know God and my family and friends will help me. I am a strong woman who is going through many hardships. I can get the information and support I need to help my daughter and myself get through this new challenge. I will be kind to myself, take care of myself, and lean on God as my strength.

Sherrie felt lighter and less burdened after connecting compassionately with herself. She did some research on the internet to help her know how to softly break the news to her daughter, found an online support group for moms of kids with diabetes, and set up an appointment for her daughter to see the doctor to get started with treatment. Being kind to herself helped Sherrie be more resilient and hopeful, and would continue to help her be an anchor for her daughter as they both tackled this new challenge.

Research shows that self-criticism is strongly linked to depression, which is linked to a lack of resilience.[3] People who are self-critical and depressed do not rebound well from the difficulties of life; instead they tend to be very self-focused as they try to survive their depression, anxiety, and the bully beating them up on the inside. Often without meaning to, self-critical people may allow their behavior and attitudes to impact others as well. The effects of living with a depressed and self-critical person can spread to family and friends.

A Friend Inside to Go through Life With

We are with ourselves 100 percent of the time. *The way you interact with yourself has a greater impact on you than any*

interactions you have with others. You have a critically important choice about whom you go through life with. Will it be
with a kind friend or a harsh inner critic? If you don't yet know
how to be your own friend, you can learn. Imagine being able
to comfort and soothe yourself through the difficulties of life.
It really is possible!

Lori felt discouraged. This was the third new church she
had tried and felt alone in. Even though people seemed to be
friendly in general, it seemed like she couldn't break into exist-
ing friendships and groups no matter how hard she tried. Lori
had tried to get into a women's small group several times, but
either wasn't called back, the timing of the group didn't work,
or she just didn't feel a part of the group. It was so confusing
for her, because in the past she'd made friends easily with the
moms of her children's friends at school and through sports.
Now that her children were in college and she had switched
churches, she felt alone and disconnected.

In an attempt to figure out what the problem was, Lori decided
it must be her. Maybe she wasn't friendly or likeable enough, or
there was something wrong with her. She was very frustrated,
shed a lot of tears, and felt like giving up. But deep down she
knew that wouldn't help, so she decided to treat herself with
kindness by telling herself some truths.

> I am a nice person who's had friends in the past. It hurts to not
> have many now, and that is a normal reaction. I think a lot of
> women feel the way I do. Over time my friendships changed
> as kids grew up, friends moved away, and I started attending
> a different church. This is a hard time for me and I'm going to
> be kind to myself rather than put myself down. I'm a loving,
> kind, and thoughtful person. It's normal for me to be frustrated
> because I am a relational person who wants to have satisfy-
> ing friendships. The problem isn't me, the problem is finding
> other women who feel similar to me, who are able to both
> give and receive.

I think I'll make an appointment with the women's director at my church and share my experience and get some ideas from her. I think I'll also join a craft class at my local craft store, and sign up for that kayaking class I've always wanted to take. God knows my need, and there is hope. I will ask him to guide me, and I will look for opportunities to be friendly and welcoming to other women who probably feel the same way I do.

Lori felt more hopeful and calm inside as she turned toward herself with understanding and compassion. How wonderful that Lori could separate *feeling* bad from *being* bad. Sometimes we get confused about this. She felt bad because of loneliness from her dwindling friendships. She comforted herself when she felt bad without making herself feel as if she were bad. By turning toward herself with compassion, she became a compassionate friend to herself. This shift can make all the difference in the world!

Get Unstuck

Often, we become stuck because we are divided against ourselves on the inside. Let's say we made a huge mistake at work, with a friend, or with our child. We are truly sorry, we have apologized, and we have done whatever we needed to correct the mistake. Yet we still blame ourselves, talk harshly to ourselves, and can't let it go. We are stuck and have an internal fight going on. The antidote to this is truth with compassion toward ourselves. Here's what you might say to yourself:

Yes, I did the wrong thing. I didn't mean to, and I am very sorry. I'm a good and imperfect person. Everyone makes mistakes, and this won't be the last one. I've done what I needed to do to apologize and make this right. My heart and intentions are good even when I make mistakes. I forgive myself, and I will let this go.

Being able to forgive ourselves for our weaknesses, mistakes, and sins is part of having a compassionate relationship with ourselves. For many of us, we are the most difficult person to forgive. We are much more able to feel compassion and understanding for others than for ourselves. Why is this? It's often because we didn't have the experience of someone giving us the gift of forgiveness or showing us *how* to forgive and be compassionate with ourselves. If we were raised in a family that tended to blame when mistakes were made rather than understand and forgive, we will have a much harder time forgiving ourselves or having a compassionate stance toward ourselves.

Here's an example that happened a number of years ago when my son was thirteen and needed to learn to forgive himself. His eleven-year-old sister was sick and trying to get some extra sleep. He had been very quiet all morning, including showering downstairs, trying not to wake her. Then he put a roll in the microwave and set the timer for three minutes instead of thirty seconds. This caused the roll to smoke and set off our very loud smoke alarm. He was very hard on himself for having done this. It was an opportunity to show him how to forgive himself in this instance.

Here's what I said to him: "Honey, you made a mistake. You never intended to set the timer to the wrong time. You never intended to set the smoke alarm off and wake up your sister. In fact, your intentions were the exact opposite. You've been very quiet getting ready this morning so you didn't wake her up. You are a kind and good boy. You just made a mistake. I know you will learn from it and double-check the timer next time. I love you and forgive you. Now you need to forgive yourself.

"Here's the truth you can tell yourself: 'I'm a good boy who cares about my sister who is sick. I did a great job getting ready so as not to wake her. I made a mistake that woke her up, but I didn't mean to. It was just a mistake. I will apologize to her and be more careful with the microwave next time. I'm a great brother.'"

Notice what it feels like to read this compassionate response. Chances are you've rarely, if ever, received this type of a response when you made a mistake, or have given yourself this type of compassionate response. The good news is that you can learn to be a kind encourager to yourself.

Here's some more help with forgiving yourself. After you have asked God to forgive you, and are "right" with him, allow some of the forgiveness he has given you to wash and cleanse you. Ask yourself some questions to highlight the truth:

- Did I do what I did on purpose?
- Am I truly sorry?
- Have I apologized and asked forgiveness from the person I hurt?
- If my friend did the same thing to someone else, would they deserve to be forgiven? What would I say to them?
- Why am I so surprised by my own sinfulness or imperfections?
- Do I really think I can go through life without making major mistakes and hurting others—even those I love?
- If I feel a nudge to take some action to make things right, what do I need in order to take the next step?

As you read these questions, don't use them to shame yourself. Use them to help you understand yourself and see if there are any steps you'd like to take to make things right regarding the situation you are thinking of. Even taking one small step is progress and growth in the right direction.

Begin to talk lovingly to yourself about what happened. Try to see yourself as God sees you (see appendix A for Bible verses about how God loves us and sees us as valuable and of great worth). Try to have empathy for yourself, without making excuses. If you need to apologize or repair a hurt, give yourself permission to do so without shame. Imagine yourself as a loving friend to the hurt part of you that can't quite forgive yourself. Come alongside yourself and consider that you can forgive yourself for the wrongs you have done. It is this type of balanced approach that allows self-compassion and truth to bring healing.

Here's some truth you might say to yourself with grace:

Dear Me,

I know you are having a really hard time forgiving yourself for what happened. I know you've tried many times to say you are forgiven, but you haven't felt forgiven. What this tells me is that you are really hurting inside about what you feel your part in this is. I'm here to tell you that you have a gracious, loving God who has forgiven you for all you have done. He is hoping and waiting for the day that you can accept his forgiveness and then extend it to yourself. Don't be surprised by how much you goof up. This is no surprise to God. He doesn't require you to not sin or to somehow be "good enough." He wants you to confess your mistakes to him, ask forgiveness from others, and work hard to turn away from the patterns of sin you fall into.

I have tears of empathy for you as I see your struggle. Some of your inability to forgive yourself may be rooted in the harmful things you did, but some of it may be shame you are carrying from something someone did to you. No matter where this shame came from, it is not too big for God to forgive or for you to forgive yourself. Maybe you aren't ready yet to forgive yourself, but my hope is that soon you will be. If you have confessed these sins to God, God looks at you with complete acceptance and love; there are no barriers between you and him. God has decided that you are forgiven, and I hope you do too. The reality is that forgiving yourself isn't really any different from forgiving someone else. Even if you've done things wrong, and even if you've caused yourself a lot of pain, you can still forgive yourself. I forgive you.

Imagine what it would be like to respond to yourself in such a compassionate way. Notice the balance of grace and truth. Yes, there is something to forgive, and yes, there is grace and understanding that can soothe and heal the regret you feel. Even if it seems impossible to speak to yourself in this way right now, please know that it is possible . . . we've just begun learning this process together. For now, allow yourself to consider that it might be possible, someday.

Concluding Reflections

As we come to the close of this first chapter, take a moment to check in with yourself about how you are doing. God gave us the ability to be aware of ourselves as well as others. He wants us to notice what is going on inside. If you would like, ponder the questions below to help process what you've read:

1. What is your response to the whole idea of having compassion for yourself?

2. What is it like to ponder that God looks at us with compassion and also wants us to approach ourselves with both compassion and truth?

3. What would it be like to go through life with a compassionate friend on the inside rather than a judging bully? In what ways would this make the biggest difference in your life?

4. Do you have trouble forgiving yourself for past mistakes and wrongs done? How might compassion toward yourself help you move toward forgiving yourself?

5. What inner reactions did you notice as you read the compassionate messages to yourself? Which one(s) in particular hit home?

2

A Look Inside

Larry had been at his new job as a department head for just three months. He couldn't believe it was happening again. Once again he felt excluded from his team. He had so much to give and could make the company so much better if they would just do things his way. Larry felt hurt that his proposals weren't being considered with the same weight as those from the other department heads, just because they had been there for twenty years. He was just as good as they were!

Larry was struggling with yet another experience that was all too familiar. This was the third workplace where he had tried to bully his way into being taken seriously, and once again his style was not well received. Because Larry was not able to see his contribution to the problem, he was destined to keep repeating this pattern wherever he went. In the process he felt wounded by his superiors' failure to wholeheartedly embrace his ideas as he also wounded countless people around him. Larry also hadn't realized that the injury he was trying to solve in his current work situation was a deep wound that had occurred when he was just a small boy.

Larry grew up in a Christian home with his parents and two brothers. His older brother was the apple of his mom's eye, and nothing Larry could do would get him the approval or sense of belonging he longed for. He spent his whole life achieving, and he became quite proficient in his career. Unfortunately, since he never got the validation and approval he craved from his mom, he sought to meet that need in his career. It was always the same . . . he was liked by coworkers one-on-one, or from a distance, but when it came to working well with others he resorted to becoming increasingly aggressive in his attempts to gain acceptance.

Because of some difficult early experiences in life, Larry felt desperate to be thought of as the best, or as special. For him, there could be only one special person. If others were equally valued, Larry saw that as a put-down. In his mind, his only recourse was to devalue and displace others as he tried to force them to give him the status and approval he desperately wanted. Because Larry felt victimized, he was unaware that his intensity to win left many of his peers feeling victimized by him.

Larry was making a mistake that many of us make: in our hurt, we neglect to notice recurring patterns in our life that indicate we are part of the problem. It may be so painful to acknowledge these recurring patterns that we look past our part and focus on how others are being so mean and unfair to us. While we may not be able to put it in words, we somehow know deep down that we will find no compassion inside if we look honestly at our part in our problems. We know that if we see the pain we bring, we may sink into a sea of self-contempt and never come out. So rather than go there, we often refuse to see what is so obvious to those around us.

Larry is experiencing the truth that when we lack compassion for ourselves, it has profoundly negative effects on us and others.

Narcissism or Self-Contempt

When we don't have a loving, compassionate relationship with ourselves, we tend to fall into two camps regarding how we handle the mistakes we make in life. If our mistakes as children were not met in a healthy way with both grace and truth, we will experience great pain when we see a mistake we've made or have a mistake brought to our attention by another. This is because we have developed no way to internally forgive ourselves and resolve the incident. We tend to either say we did nothing wrong at all and it was all the other person's fault (narcissism), or say we are the worst person in the world and we don't deserve to be forgiven (shame and self-contempt).

This happens because we never learned how to forgive ourselves for our part in the situation. This lack of self-compassion causes significant problems in our relationships. We may find it hard to resolve problems by taking the steps necessary to repair the normal hurts that occur in all relationships. In an attempt to not experience pain, we come up with every reason possible to not see or own up to the mistake we made. Here's what tends to happen:

1. Others are afraid to bring anything up because we will either refuse to accept responsibility for our part or fall into a deep hole of shame. Both of these keep us self-focused and don't address the other person's concerns.

2. Others take the risk to bring up a problem but end up confused and hurt when their issues are never taken seriously. The conversation either shifts to how awful *we feel* about what happened or we spend time defending our actions. We

29

don't acknowledge the hurt we caused, even if unintended, offer an apology, or take steps to make things right.

Not only do these responses hurt our relationships but they also cause problems for us. If we can't acknowledge in a healthy way where we erred, there is no possibility of changing, learning, and growing. When this happens, we don't learn from our mistakes, and we keep repeating them over and over again—resulting in more and more pain and loneliness.

Fake Repentance versus Real Repentance

There is a big difference between fake repentance and real repentance. Fake repentance involves the person being sad, upset, angry, or distraught when confronted with actions or inactions that were hurtful. She is upset that you and others might not see her positively, that you are disappointed in her, that you view her in a negative way, and so forth.

Real repentance may look the same on the outside; however, what differs is the *reason* the person is upset about what she did. When people are truly repentant, they are sorry because they sinned, they hurt you, they hurt the trust in the relationship, or they did something they knew was wrong.

Notice the difference. Fake repentance is about how the mistake makes me look bad and how others will see me differently. Real repentance is about how I've sinned, how I've hurt you, or how I violated my own moral values. Fake repentance is about me, and real repentance is about you and repairing the hurt I've caused.

Self-compassion helps us be truly repentant when we see our mistakes or are confronted by another person. We can see ourselves as someone who is created by God and has many strengths but who made a mistake or sinned and needs to repent. When we see ourselves in this balanced way—with truth and grace—we can acknowledge our faults without either falling into a self-focused pit of shame or defending against seeing the truth of the situation.

Before you start getting down on yourself for responding in unhealthy ways, you can talk to yourself with compassion:

> I think I sometimes do respond in these ways when someone tries to share a problem with me. I don't mean to. When someone tells me I've hurt them or criticizes me, I start to hurt on the inside and I lose sight of the other person and their hurt. I realize now it is because I was never taught how to respond in healthy ways that show concern for the other person and myself at the same time. I have felt I need to either defend myself and convince the other person I'm not bad or take all the blame and see myself as awful. I realize now that neither of these ways of responding are accurate or healthy, and they cause me to lose sight of the other person. It seems impossible right now to think of responding differently, but I know I can learn. It's not too late. I'm a valuable person with flaws, and God loves me and accepts me.

Let's take a moment to revisit Larry and the stuck place he's found himself in. Fortunately for Larry, a longtime childhood friend, Bill, took a risk to share with him the pattern he'd seen over the last thirty years. Larry was defensive at first. Because Bill grew up with Larry he was able to share with him the pain he'd seen Larry go through as he worked so hard to get love and approval from his mom. As Bill shared, Larry could feel those awful feelings of shame and rejection coming up again. In his effort not to feel those feelings again, he would push others in high places to validate his worth and elevate him to the top spot no matter what. If he could get them to do this, he wouldn't have to feel the devastating shame he carried. As Bill gently shared these observations, Larry felt a slight softening on the inside. Bill was helping Larry see how he might be part of his current problem, and he was doing it with compassion, not judgment or rejection. Larry was at a crossroads. He could stay in his defensive stance of "It's everyone else's fault but mine, and I'm the victim here," or he could consider changing paths by getting help to deal with his narcissism. Bill shared that this was such an ingrained pattern in Larry that he would need the help of a therapist, a lot of time, and lots of self-compassion. If Larry opted to take this healthier though very scary path, he might say something like this to himself:

> Wow . . . I can't believe what Bill told me. I'm scared he's just like everyone else . . . wanting me to admit all this is my fault. I'm really touched by the way he talked to me. Even though what he said was really painful, I could tell that he really cares about me and the hard time I'm having. He was right that I've had this pain inside me my whole life. I can't remember a time when I haven't felt rejected and not good enough. It seems like I'm always fighting to get people at work to see my value and recognize that I'm important and special. It just hurts so much. I can clearly see how others are hurting me, but I don't see how he says I'm hurting them. After hearing what Bill said, maybe I do have a tiny part in the difficulties at work too. This is so hard to figure out. Maybe it would help to talk to someone.

If Larry chooses this healthy path and sticks with it, he will make a courageous choice. It is tough but possible to heal this kind of ingrained wound. There is hope in this choice, whereas there is no hope in the defensive choice of trying to convince yourself that you have no part in your difficulties . . . all while watching your life and relationships fall apart.

Disconnection and Loneliness

When we aren't able to respond to ourselves with compassion, we feel very disconnected from ourselves. When normal mistakes and weaknesses are met with a lack of compassion and forgiveness by others, an inner critic develops inside that views our own mistakes in this harsh way as well. This will cause us to feel lonely inside because we have no inner ally in times of trouble. This is so opposite of how God looks at us. He has a soft heart toward our tender, breaking hearts. He is our ally in times of trouble, and we can model his attitude and stance toward us.

> God is our refuge and strength,
> an ever-present help in trouble. (Ps. 46:1)

Imagine how different your internal world will be when you are able to join with God in being a present help to yourself in times of trouble.

Our Emotional and Relational Needs

We were all born with emotional, physical, relational, and spiritual needs. Ideally our parents and caregivers met these needs when we were small. Most parents are wonderful about meeting their child's physical needs for food, shelter, clothes, schooling, and so on. But besides these basic needs, we also have vital emotional, relational, and spiritual needs that often get missed, usually because those who raised us never had these met themselves. These needs are on a continuum. Some may have been met very well, and some not. Some may have been met by one parent but not the other. Some may have been met by a teacher, neighbor, friend, or pastor who took a real interest in you.

It is important to understand yourself and which of your needs were met. This reflection will help you develop compassion for yourself, rather than blame or criticism for others. Later, chapter 6 will help you assess your needs more completely and help you come up with a plan to meet them. While this exercise looks at childhood needs, these same needs are also important in adult relationships.

Eye Contact

This is one of the most important ways of communicating love, especially to young children. Children suck in nurturing love through eye contact. It is important for a child to receive eye contact *consistently*, regardless of behavior. If a child only receives eye contact when the parent is angry ("Look at me when I'm talking to you.") the child may come to fear relational closeness. If a child only receives eye contact when the child "performs well" they will learn that love is conditional.

Physical Touch

Physical touch fills children's emotional and relational tanks. A hug, a kiss, holding hands, a touch on the shoulder, or a pat on the head all convey love in a tangible way that a child can feel and soak in. As children get older, they may want love expressed in different ways, such as a back scratch, a pat on the back or shoulder, wrestling, or sitting close while watching television. These ways of expressing love communicate the message that "You're loved. You're accepted. You matter. I want to be close to you."

Focused Attention

Children need times of full, undivided attention in such a way that they feel without a doubt that they are completely loved. This experience makes children feel of great worth and value and is vital to good self-esteem and the ability to relate to and love others. Children do not do their best, feel their best, or behave their best unless they are given focused attention. Making this happen is worth the effort, because without it children feel anxiety as they get the sense that everything else is more important than they are.

Playtime

Children need time to play with their parents and caregivers. Unstructured time to play whatever the child wants gives important messages that are soaked deep into the soul: "You are loved. You are worth the time. You are more important than other things. I care about what matters to you."

Older children may enjoy watching a favorite show together, showing you a part of a favorite video game, sitting side-by-side on the back step, taking a walk, or sweating it out on the basketball court. When children share their interests and are responded to with curiosity and attention, they feel known and loved. With this warm, trusting, loving relationship in place, children are able to handle the many challenges they face at school, with friends, and in life.

Validation with Empathy

This way of interacting is one of the most powerful ways that children experience love and worth. As parents put themselves in their children's shoes, and wonder what it must be like to be that child in a given situation, children experience that they really matter. When children believe their thoughts and feelings matter, they will feel connected to their parents on a heart level. Validation with empathy involves reflecting back the facts and feelings of what children shared without trying to fix the problem.

As Gary and Joy Lundberg say in *I Don't Have to Make Everything All Better*, validation with empathy helps meet children's universal need

> to know that I have worth, my feelings matter, and someone really cares about me. . . . All of us want to be listened to and

understood. We want to be appreciated for who we are individually. We need to be heard completely and not judged, corrected, or advised. When those who are meaningful to us will not take the time to hear us out by genuinely listening, we experience a profound negative effect.[1]

Making Choices

Allowing children to make some of their own choices gives them a real experience that they are trusted and that they can come to trust themselves as well. Even when children's choices are wrong, great learning can occur. Of even greater importance, children can learn to not fear their mistakes and know that mistakes can be repaired and relationships restored.

Safe and Secure Routine

Children's anxiety and insecurities decrease when they can depend on a routine that allows them to anticipate what will happen next. They benefit from knowing that "this is what the plan is," as well as that it can be flexibly adjusted if necessary.

Clear Boundaries and Limits

When children are parented with natural, logical consequences they will be secure in knowing what will happen regarding their choices and behavior. Children who experience inconsistent discipline feel anxious and insecure.

Help Managing Emotions

Knowing how to manage emotions does not come naturally. Children need help identifying and naming their emotions in order to express them in healthy ways. In addition, children need help learning to soothe themselves and return their body to equilibrium when distressed.

Protection from Harm

Children need to be protected from harm as much as possible. They are young and vulnerable and have not yet developed the skills they need to protect themselves. It is not possible to protect children from every possible harmful event, but there are many things that parents can do to help with prevention. Children need to be protected from known neglect as well as physical, emotional, spiritual, and sexual abuse inside or outside the home.

Spiritual Needs

Children deserve to be introduced to a loving and caring God. We are made with a place inside that wants and needs to connect to him. Parents, especially those who do not actively participate in their own faith community, may overlook this aspect of their children's development. Spiritual practices can help children develop into healthy people who are able to cope with life's difficulties and stresses.

Special Words of Compassion for Parents

As you contemplate your own needs growing up, no doubt you are thinking about what needs you did or did not meet for your own children. Please keep the following in mind if you are feeling regret: it is impossible to meet all the needs of a child. If a parent's specific need has not been met as a child, that parent will not have an instinctual ability to meet that need for their child. It is never too late to try to repair any such unintentional hurts. Your child is in God's hands, and God is gracious to use both our successes and mistakes with our children to help them grow. We deeply love our children, and that love is a foundation for them. Here are some compassionate statements you can say to yourself in this regard:

This section on childhood needs really struck me. It helped me understand different areas I've struggled with as I contemplate how many of my needs were not met growing up. I feel compassion for myself as I see what an uphill battle I've had to fight without the resources and skills I've needed. It also causes pangs of guilt as I realize that I also didn't meet all the needs my children had. On the one hand I feel so much regret for all I didn't know about meeting some of my children's needs. On the other hand I know there was no way I could know how to meet certain needs when they were not met for me growing up. I want to take the time to process my feelings in a journal or with a trusted friend. I will pray and consider how and when to talk to my children about different regrets I have, and I will give them a chance to share with me their own experiences. I know this may not be possible, but I am open to ways I might repair that relationship. I know my children are in God's hands, and he will use both the positives and negatives of my parenting to shape them. I have no doubt of my love for my children, and I know they can feel that deep down. I will try to extend compassion to myself for the pain I am feeling. As I heal in this process, I can become more emotionally trustworthy as a person and a parent. With God's help, this can be the beginning of building a new foundation of love and trust with my children as well as with myself.

The Result of Unmet Needs

When children's needs for love, affirmation, approval, nurturing, and protection are not met to a "good enough" level, they will come to see their needs as bad or wrong.[2] When this happens, there are only two conclusions they can make:

1. My needs aren't being met because my needs are wrong or bad, and/or there is something wrong with me and I'm "not enough."
2. My needs aren't being met because my parents either don't want to meet them or are unable or incapable of meeting them.

Children almost always believe number one for two important reasons. One, developmentally they are at a stage where they see themselves at the center of everything. This isn't from a place of selfishness; it is a developmental issue. They can't see that other people are the cause of things—just themselves. It is part of the brain-wiring limitations of early childhood.

Two, it is much safer emotionally for them to believe number one. That may come as a surprise. Children will feel very scared as well as powerless if they believe that their parents won't or can't meet some of their basic needs. They are 100 percent dependent on their parents because they are children. To believe that the people you are completely counting on don't have it in them to meet your needs is terrifying.

It is less scary for children to believe that the reason their needs aren't being met is because of some problem in themselves. If they believe this, their anxiety and feelings of powerlessness decrease because at least they think they can do something about it. And so begins a lifelong journey of working hard, caring for others, suppressing their own needs, and trying to be perfect or funny or beautiful or athletic or smart in the hope of getting those needs met.

This "work harder" strategy never succeeds, because the reason their needs weren't met in the first place was about the pain and limitations of those raising them, not because of a defect in themselves. Their needs weren't met because they had imperfect parents who had imperfect parents. As a result children never realize that their needs are good, and that in fact they are God-given—placed in us by our Creator.

This striving to do whatever is necessary to have our unmet needs met continues into adulthood as we keep trying to win love, affirmation, approval, and nurturing. Unfortunately what also continues is a disdain for our needs. We feel as if our needs make us weak, pathetic, disgusting, or burdensome to others.

This is where self-compassion comes in. As we take this new understanding and look back on the conclusions we made as children, we can have compassion for that poor little child who was doing the best they could do at the time. We can also look with compassion and grace at the unsuccessful ways we've tried to meet these needs as an adult. This doesn't absolve us from sin or hurt we've caused to ourselves or others. It does explain a lot about how and why we tried what we did to get those needs met and helps us to extend compassion to ourselves about the previous choices we've made. This leads us to meet these needs in healthy ways as well as repair any damage done to others and ourselves. If this section speaks to you, here are some compassionate words you might say to yourself:

> I had no idea that the conclusion I made as a child—that my needs were bad—was the only conclusion a child could make. Because I made it so long ago it seems true. I realize now that it was way too scary for me to see that the problem wasn't with me. I was just a child, vulnerable and meant to be cared for. There's nothing wrong with that. I'm going to ponder this new information—that my needs are God-given and good. This feels new and in some way wrong because I've believed I was the problem for so long. At the same time it feels hopeful because somewhere inside I know what I just learned is true.
>
> What a new concept . . . that I can recognize that the past ways I've tried to meet my needs were unhealthy and at the same time have compassion for myself for being placed in that situation. I'm realizing that I was not prepared to handle the difficulties of life. I was thrown into life without tools or skills, and I did the best I could to figure things out. In the process I've been hurt and have hurt others, but this came from a place of not knowing. It is good to know now why I keep struggling with the same situations over and over. I will continue to take steps to grow in the areas I've never had a chance to develop, as well as take steps to right any wrongs I've caused.

Overdependence on Others' Validation

It is normal to desire validation and feel good when others validate you. I feel all warm and fuzzy inside when someone tells me she appreciates me or values what I've done for her. There is nothing wrong with welcoming this kind of encouragement. It only becomes problematic when we *only* have others as the source of our encouragement and validation.

When this is the case, it causes us to be dependent upon others for our well-being. Without meaning to, we frequently seek affirmation from others, which can pressure them to make us feel good. It can also place us in a position of trying to please others so that we can get affirmation, all the while ignoring our own instincts and needs as well as how God might be speaking to us.

The Waiting Stance

When we aren't caring for ourselves, no amount of encouragement or care from another person is enough. So we wait. We are often taught to look for just the right friend or spouse who will meet our needs perfectly, to the exclusion of our own responsibility in meeting our needs. We get this message from many sources including fairy tales, movies, television shows, and advertisements, as well as from family and friends. We are also often taught in church that God will meet all of our needs, to the exclusion of our responsibility to be active in caring for ourselves as well. A healthy balance is to understand that we, as Christians, are influenced by God's presence and direction in our life. At the same time we are also responsible and equipped by God to care for ourselves and all he has given us.

When we are stuck in a waiting stance, we can often become bitter, resentful, and passive as we wait for that "other," often including God, to step in and meet our needs. It's as if we have our arms crossed on the inside, just waiting for someone to come through—all while taking little or no action on our own behalf.

Mary was very discouraged. She hated her job and felt like God had more for her. She'd worked at a fast-food restaurant for fifteen years and didn't enjoy dealing with customers, which was exactly what her job entailed. She'd prayed about it and asked her friends to pray that God would get her a new job . . . for twelve years! She couldn't understand why God wasn't acting on her behalf, and he felt far away from her. She knew she liked working with numbers and not so much with people. She had taken two accounting classes at her local community college and felt like this was the kind of work she could be good at and would enjoy.

Mary did a lot of positive things in noticing what she liked and didn't like, in taking two classes, and in enlisting prayer on her behalf. The problem was that Mary was in a waiting stance. She was waiting for God to plop a job in her lap . . . and it appeared that God did not agree with her plan. Mary neglected actively applying for other jobs, interviewing accountants in the area for advice, or volunteering to help with accounting at her church, for example. Besides the hardships of working at a job that she hated, the greater cost was starting to show in her relationship with God and her own mounting depression. In her church, Mary had been taught this "magical thinking" that God would just provide, but no one shared with her that she needed to take an active role as well.

This new way of thinking—that we are responsible and given the task to be active in meeting our needs with God's leading and provision—can be a very tough shift for some to make. It will be especially difficult if our basic needs for love, caring, and protection weren't met growing up. Sometimes when we've been in this situation, we stay in a waiting stance without even knowing it: waiting for our husband, wife, friend, boss, girlfriend, boyfriend, or parents to give us what we need. In our quest to find that perfect person to meet our needs, we neglect the relationship with ourselves.

As Mary realized she was in a waiting stance, she was able to speak to herself with both grace and truth:

> I'm coming to realize that without knowing it I have been waiting for God to magically change my work situation. I've taken some good steps, but realize that I need to be even more active in finding another job. Even though I'd rather have God plop one in my lap, he must want me to be more involved in the process. I feel better just realizing this. I've been told since I was in Sunday school that God would provide, but no one explained that I also have an active part to play. Even though it is a little scary to think of taking action, it is also exciting. I have several ideas I can try this week. I can be compassionate to myself about the stuck place I've been in and also feel relieved that I can intentionally move forward.

It is very common not to realize you are in a waiting stance. God created us uniquely with a passion and a purpose. He wants us to be active in our lives. Consider this famous verse:

> But they that wait upon the LORD shall renew their strength; they shall mount up with wings as eagles; they shall run, and not be weary; and they shall walk, and not faint. (Isa. 40:31 KJV)

This Scripture is written in an active tense: we are being encouraged to be active in our own lives while waiting on God's direction and leading. Notice how active the verbs are in this verse (mount up, run, walk).

Caring for ourselves is an active process. We can learn how to be trustworthy with ourselves—to listen to our instincts, needs, and wants while also listening to God's leading and guidance.

Here's a way to be compassionate with yourself in this regard:

> I didn't fully realize I've been on "pause," waiting for my needs for caring and compassion to be met by someone else. On the one hand, I'm not crazy about the idea that it is up to me

to find ways to care for my unmet needs. On the other hand, it is good news to know that it isn't selfish for me to listen to the instincts God's put in me. It is a little exciting, although foreign, to think of valuing my own needs as well as others. I'll give myself time to ponder this and try out a few things.

Concluding Reflections

As we come to the close of this chapter, take a moment to check in with yourself about how you are doing. If you would like, ponder the questions below to help process what you've read:

1. What was your response as you read about our tendency to fall into narcissism or self-contempt when faced with our mistakes? Where do you see yourself in this dilemma?

2. Have you ever experienced someone responding to your mistakes with compassion? If so, who was it, and what was this experience like? If not, what might it be like to become that person for yourself?

3. What were your thoughts and feelings when you read about your normal "needs"?

4. Which of your needs were met growing up? (circle them)

   eye contact   physical touch   focused attention
   playtime   validation with empathy
   making choices   clear boundaries
   safe and secure routine   spiritual instruction
   help managing emotions   protection from harm

5. How do you view your needs now? What is something compassionate you could say to yourself about your needs, and how might you take steps to meet them now?

3

Why It Is So Hard
to Be Compassionate
with Ourselves

Most people find it hard to show compassion to themselves. It is tough to approach oneself with a stance of grace and truth. What I mean by that is:

Grace is compassion toward yourself with kindness and gentleness.

Truth is acknowledging the truth of the situation, but without shame.

Grace and truth together mean you acknowledge what happened without either minimizing it or making it more than it was, and at the same time apply compassion to yourself. It is difficult to have compassion for yourself when hard things happen or if you missed important nurturing experiences.

Modeling Compassion

In order to know how to be compassionate with ourselves, we need to experience receiving compassion as well as watch other people treat themselves with compassion. If we had few personal experiences or models to watch, that place inside where we learn to be compassionate with ourselves doesn't develop naturally. The good news: it still can!

Let me give you an example of a situation in which I really let someone down and how I treated myself with grace and truth regarding this failing.

A few years ago I dropped the ball on being supportive to my sister, who is disabled from a serious illness. I intended to call her frequently since she was going through surgery and recovery and she lived four hundred miles away. But I didn't follow through. This hurt her greatly and caused a rift in our relationship that we had to work through. The back story to this situation was that two other people dear to me were going through very serious crises as well, and it was all I could do to keep my head above water. No excuses—that's what was happening.

When I became aware of how much I had hurt my sister, I felt horrible. It took a while to work through it. This is what I said to myself:

> I really dropped the ball and hurt my sister. I never intended to. I love her and want to always be a support to her. I also recognize that I was being pulled in several other directions by two simultaneous crises in the lives of people right here that have taken my focus and energy. Most people in my situation would not have been able to provide as much support as I did. At the same time I really hurt my sister, and I need to make it right. My dropping the ball doesn't make me a bad person. It makes me a human person who was stretched way too thin.

Here's what I said to her: "I am so sorry for not being there for you when you needed me. I wanted to be there for you, and I feel horrible for letting you down. I love and value you, and I know I really hurt you a lot. I want to work through this with you. Will you please forgive me?"

After I listened to her hurt feelings and what it was like for her, I later asked her if I could share what had been going on in my life that was a part of the picture. I did this not as a way of offering an excuse but as a way to let her know my neglect was not because I didn't care about her. I explained that I was in the middle of two simultaneous "tornadoes," and as we talked it through, she understood and had compassion for me as well.

I learned a valuable lesson from this. Even at times when I'm feeling overwhelmed, I can still take a moment to let other people in my life who depend on me know what's going on. This way they are clued in and won't experience my lessened involvement as a personal rejection.

Repeated Criticism

Repeated criticism creates a challenge because we may have internalized and accepted critical messages we heard growing up. A part of us has taken on a "bully" stance toward our mistakes, weaknesses, and areas of sin. We were not taught a different motivation to change besides being hard on ourselves. Believe it or not, there are other reasons that can motivate us to grow and change:

- Wanting to be the most honorable and caring person possible.
- Not wanting to hurt others.
- Wanting to show honor to God by becoming as spiritually, relationally, and emotionally healthy as possible.
- Wanting to be a safe and trustworthy person in our relationships.
- Wanting to grow in order to fulfill our potential.

These reasons are in direct contrast to trying to change because we see ourselves as bad, as a loser, or as a misfit. One important thing to realize: this "bully" inside is actually trying to help in the only way it knows how. These good intentions attempt to keep us out of trouble, help us perform well, and not be lazy, to name a few. These harsh strategies developed when we were young and often carry into adulthood. How wonderful it is, now, to learn new ways to motivate ourselves that are healthy, not harmful. Imagine what it would be like to respond to ourselves with compassion rather than judgment.

Eric was one set down in the finals of his college tennis championship. He was really stressed and wanted to win the match. He was a senior and wouldn't have this chance again. It was great that his family and friends were in the stands, but it also increased the pressure he felt. He started talking to himself harshly. *You're so lame! How could you miss that last shot? You do so much better at practice, then you fall apart when it really matters.* This way of talking to himself was a habit modeled to him by his coach, who thought harshness and shame were great motivators. This didn't work for Eric. He felt worse and made more mistakes when he treated himself harshly. He took a deep breath and decided to talk to himself a little more kindly. Just *deciding* to befriend himself brought down his tension a bit. As he prepared to receive his opponent's serve, he said to himself, *You can do this. You've practiced hard and know how to handle this pressure. Just take one ball at a time and do what you do. I know what a good player you are. You can do this!* It was amazing to him how these words of kindness and confidence helped him to focus and settle down. He played well the rest of the match, and he was proud of himself for finishing strong and being a compassionate coach to himself.

As you hear Eric's story, you may want to talk to yourself compassionately about the ways you tend to be harsh with yourself:

Yes, I do tend to be really hard on myself. I say horrible things to myself to try to get myself to do the right thing. Sometimes, I even punish myself on purpose for being such a mess-up. I didn't realize until now that I can relate to myself in a different way. I actually feel some compassion for that small bullying part of me that had to develop to keep me out of trouble.

Although I can't even imagine trying to motivate myself to change because of positive reasons, I am starting to believe maybe it's possible. I guess it makes sense that if I never had a model of how to be both truthful and compassionate with myself at the same time, I wouldn't know how to do it. I have a little spark of hope that I can learn a different way.

Solid Emotional Connections

A bond between two people is an emotional and intellectual investment they have in one another. It is a relationship in which all of the parts of the soul—feelings, thoughts, values, beliefs, joys, and sorrows—are shared with and valued by another. . . . The best way to define bonding at its core is to say that when I am bonded, I "matter" to someone. When we are bonded to someone, we feel that we make a difference to him, that our presence is desired when we are around and missed when we are absent. This sense of "mattering" is in direct contrast to feeling overlooked, forgotten, or even simply tolerated by others.[1]

That is quite a quote, isn't it? Many people have not had the experience of feeling bonded or connected to others in this way. Because of this, there is a whole field of psychology that studies not only the different types of attachments or bonds we form with one another but also the effects when they do not form securely.

This attachment theory helps explain the comfort we have or don't have with people and relationships based upon our own experiences of feeling safe and loved as children. Following is a

brief synopsis of this theory and how it may relate to the connection we feel with others.[2]

> We are made to be in relationships—close, connected, mutu-
> ally supportive relationships.
>
> We have this need from the beginning of life until we die.
>
> When we are not in these types of safe and supportive re-
> lationships, we suffer in many ways. These areas include
> emotional and physical health, spiritual health, and psy-
> chological and behavioral health. Symptoms include alone-
> ness, difficulties handling stress, relationship problems,
> acting out, depression, anxiety, and addictions.
>
> The way we think, the beliefs and feelings we have, and what
> we do are shaped by the early experiences of bonding and
> attachment we experienced as small children.
>
> How lovable we see ourselves, as well as how responsive and
> capable we are in loving others, is deeply affected by how
> our needs were responded to when we were young.

Stated simply, when our needs for love, affection, food, comfort,
physical needs, and protection are met to a "good enough" level,
we will come away with a conclusion that we are lovable, and that
others are trustworthy and able to meet our needs. This is called
secure attachment. Those with secure attachment believe they are
worthy of love and that others are able and willing to meet their
needs. They are comfortable with both closeness and independence.

However, when these needs are not met, and/or if emotional,
sexual, or physical abuse and neglect occur, a person will experience *insecure attachment*. There are three types of ways people
relate to themselves and others when they have not experienced
secure attachment growing up:

1. Those who experience anxiety in relationships tend to
   see themselves in a negative light (flawed, helpless, and

"less than") and see others in an overly positive light ("all together" and able to fix things for them). They tend to desire relationships but feel anxious about them. They fear abandonment because they don't see themselves as worthy of love, and they expect to be cast aside. They are often very critical of themselves and have little ability to comfort, nurture, or soothe themselves.

2. Those who shy away from or avoid relationships tend to see themselves in an overly positive light and see others in an overly negative light. They feel uncomfortable with closeness and can be overly self-reliant. They expect that others will not be there for them or they are impossible to please. They do not possess the skills and internal connection to bring comfort and support to themselves.

3. Those who experience fear in relationships see both themselves and others in a negative light. They experience the double whammy of being disconnected and untrusting of themselves and others. They feel uncomfortable with closeness and often steer away from relationships altogether. Most of life is spent just trying to survive. They do not know how to provide themselves with kindness, comfort, and care.

How do these attachment styles relate to developing a compassionate relationship with yourself? In the three types of insecure attachment (anxious, avoidant, and fearful), we become disconnected from ourselves in a variety of ways. When things are difficult as a child, it is normal to push difficult feelings away (emotional disconnection), blame ourselves for what went wrong (distorted view of self), and establish coping skills to get us through (usually unhealthy, as we don't know what else to do). Even if we were fortunate enough to be raised in a securely attached home, difficult experiences in adulthood can still happen. These can also shake up our secure attachment and affect our view of ourselves.

The vast majority of people have experienced wounding in the way they view and connect with themselves. We can all benefit from giving ourselves a break by developing a compassionate relationship with ourselves. Part of our healing and growth is to repair the division that has happened inside ourselves, whether that be a negative or overly positive view of ourselves, a disconnection with our feelings and needs, or a lack of self-care.

Mixed Messages

It breaks my heart to see people hurt because they've been taught that God looks down on them. That is not true! God sent his Son, Jesus, to die for our sins and pay that price. He doesn't want or expect us to be wallowing in the shame of our wrongdoings. He doesn't want us to try to pay for the salvation he's already purchased. This is the gift of God's grace and mercy freely given at salvation.

God wants us to receive his gift of salvation and then depend on him to live out the life he's given us in the best way possible. He does grieve when we sin, but not for the reasons we are often told. He grieves because it puts a barrier between us and him that we need to work through. He grieves because he knows there are natural consequences we will have to go through, work through, and repair. He loves us. He hurts with us just as you do when you see your child do something wrong that will have consequences at school or with friends. In the same way that you would never think of disowning your child, he *never* thinks of disowning or abandoning us. He has compassion for us, and he wants us to have compassion for ourselves as well.

> When Jesus landed and saw a large crowd, he had compassion on them, because they were like sheep without a shepherd. So he began teaching them many things. (Mark 6:34)

Notice that the verse doesn't say that he had contempt for them. *Why don't they have a shepherd? What's wrong with them?* No, it says he saw their predicament, had compassion, and sought to meet their need. If you've been taught incorrectly about God's compassion, you can say to yourself:

> Wow, I never learned about how God has compassion about weakness and needs. He doesn't have contempt for these human traits the way I do. I wish I'd known this sooner, and now I can learn more about this if I want. Because I was taught incorrectly doesn't mean I'm bad or stupid, it just means I was taught some things about God by someone who didn't know either. I can learn to view my needs and weaknesses the way God does.

Fearing Compassion

Sometimes we fear that compassion equals self-pity, or we are afraid that if we are compassionate with ourselves we will go completely out of control. Let's take that idea one piece at a time. Many people think that self-compassion equals looking at oneself with pity. For some, *pity* is a negative word. They see it as looking at oneself as a pathetic and sorry excuse for a person. That isn't self-compassion; it is self-disdain. Self-compassion is looking at our humanness and our situation with empathy, concern, and kindness.

Self-compassion is also pausing to look back and feel compassion for the difficult times you've been through. Life is hard even in the best of families or situations. No one can stop sin; hardships; the effects of mental illness, abuse, or neglect; or the effects of living in a busy, mixed-up world. As you think about this now, allow yourself to have the understanding and compassion for yourself that you would have for a small, struggling child. Each of us is the product of genetics, life experiences, temperament, flawed people, and our own imperfections. Take a moment to let in a little compassion for yourself right now.

The other confusion about having compassion for ourselves is being afraid that doing so would be a license to sin and go wild. While I can understand that concern, the opposite is actually true. When we don't have self-compassion (and instead carry a lot of self-contempt and self-criticism), we feel a lot of deep hurt and shame. These feelings are so painful that we can rarely tolerate them for long. We push them down, but eventually they come up—and usually with a fury. When we are in this state of emotional pain without a way to process these feelings, we will do anything to not feel them. This is when we are most likely to sin or act out our pain through negative behaviors and addictions.

Self-compassion doesn't take away the sin, the mistake, or the need to change. It soothes the hurt and self-contempt. This soothing makes us less likely to act out our pain through our behaviors.

Jane had snapped at her three kids again. She hated being so impatient with them and seeing their little hurt faces and tears when she snapped at them, but it seemed like they had an unending series of needs for her to meet. One wanted her to play Barbies, one wanted to tell her what happened at school that day, and one wanted her to rush to the store to buy what was needed for a school project that was due tomorrow.

Jane was just one person. She loved her children dearly and thanked God every day for being able to stay home with them. At the same time, sometimes she wanted to run away and let someone else figure out all the meals, laundry, homework, cleaning, and never-ending questions. Her kids had it so much better than she did as a child. Her parents were gone a lot, and she pretty much raised herself and her younger brother. Her kids didn't know how good they had it or how hard it had been for her growing up.

Jane decided that both she and her kids were having a tough day, and they all needed a break. As she took a few slow deep breaths to calm herself, she said, "It's normal for me to be exhausted taking care of my kids. It's normal for me to want a break and to want them to appreciate all I do for them. It's also normal for them to be little kids and not think about all that. I can have compassion for myself and all I went through growing up. It was painful and lonely at times, and I would have loved a mom like me who was able to put so much into her kids. I will also have compassion for myself now, being a stay-at-home mom of three small children. I will remember that my children also deserve compassion for the normal frustrations they experience as well as for sometimes dealing with a crabby mom."

If you see yourself in this section, you can show compassion to yourself by saying the following:

> I am so glad to hear that self-compassion isn't pity, and it doesn't give me a reason to act out. I'm going to try to think about being compassionate to myself as a balanced way of acknowledging my weaknesses, needs, and sin. I'm so glad that God isn't repulsed by my struggles, and I'm going to start to treat myself in a kinder way too. This is such a new way of thinking and responding to myself. It feels good and strange at the same time. I can learn how to show more compassion to myself.

Mistakes Are Normal

Some of us were never taught that mistakes are normal and should be handled with grace toward ourselves. The reality is that every part of life is a learning curve. It is that way from the moment we enter the world until the day we die. Therefore everyone needs to come up with a grace- and truth-filled way of handling our frequent inevitable failures. It's not too late. I don't know about you, but I mainly learn from the mistakes I make and from adjusting to the curveballs life throws at me.

When our children were young, I was struck by the fact that everything they were learning was new—everything. Every day they were learning twenty-plus new things because they'd never done them before. That meant lots of learning—and lots of failing. I wanted to help them learn new things, but more importantly I wanted them to learn how to be kind to themselves when they wouldn't get things quite right.

This is true for every age. I had never been a mom before, so I was on a constant learning curve. As soon as I'd figured out how to mother a baby, I had to figure out how to mother both an eighteen-month-old and a newborn. Life is a constant cycle of learning, failing, learning, growing, and so on. I'm still on a learning curve and will be until the day I die. So will you.

If we grew up in a family where this basic truth was not known and/or embraced, we have most likely come away with messages such as: "It is wrong to make mistakes," "We should know how to do everything," or "You're bad when you make a mistake." As a child you aren't able to step back and say to yourself, *It's normal for me to spill milk. I have little hands, and my eye-hand coordination isn't very good yet, which is typical for a child my age. Mom and Dad, why are you so upset over something that is normal and expected?*

Little kids don't have the ability to think about a situation in this way, so instead they accept shame about making normal mistakes and other failures as gospel truth. Over time, a place develops inside us that really believes *I'm bad or wrong for making this mistake.* What doesn't develop is self-compassion for being a little guy or gal (all the way through being an adult) and how tough it is to not know everything yet be expected to.

So a new way to respond to all of our inevitable mistakes and failures is this: Rather than beat ourselves up for what we did do, didn't do, should have done, should have known, and so forth, how about learning from each situation while having compassion for how difficult it was to go through?

In my experience, one of the only ways to ease the pain of disappointment, hurt, or confusion is soothing comfort. When we know someone else sees us, cares about what we are going through, and expresses that to us, it eases our pain. Just imagine how nice it could be if you become that comforting and soothing voice for yourself.

If you can relate to this section, it explains why you may have trouble being kind to yourself when you "mess up." I can't imagine how you would know how to respond to yourself any other way. Take heart, you can learn! Here's something caring you could say to yourself now:

> Wow, I'm starting to realize why I'm so hard on myself. It makes sense. I was never taught how normal and expected it is to make mistakes and not know things. I always thought I was bad or wrong for this. It turns out I was normal! I'm going to breathe in this new truth: it is normal for me to make mistakes, and it doesn't make me a bad or "less than" person. I'm going to learn how to let some of that shame wash away and allow myself to learn from the normal mistakes I make and the learning curves I'm on.

Concluding Reflections

As we come to the close of this chapter, take a moment to check in with yourself about how you are doing. If you would like, ponder the questions below to help process what you've read:

1. What is your response to hearing all the valid reasons why it is difficult to be compassionate with yourself? Which one(s) really hit home?

2. What compassionate words do you need to say to yourself about difficult experiences you've been through as a child, teenager, or adult?

3. In what ways can you look on this bully part of you with a bit of compassion? How does it feel to begin to understand that this bully has only been doing what he/she knows in order to keep you from getting into trouble?

4. What reactions inside did you notice as you read Eric's and Jane's compassionate messages to themselves, as well as the other compassionate self-statements in this chapter?

5. Try a compassion moment by soaking in past times of receiving compassion:

   a. Get comfortable and relaxed, and remember a time when you felt someone have compassion for you (friend, God, family member, coworker, teacher, counselor, pastor). You can also think of a time you saw compassion expressed to another person.

   b. Notice what it felt like for that person to see you and have compassion for you and what you were going through. Notice the thoughts and feelings you had and how it feels in your body to remember it now.

   c. Allow yourself to soak that compassion in at an even deeper level. Breathe it in through your whole body.

   d. Allow a little of that compassion to come from you to yourself as well. Breathe it in through your whole body.

   e. Attach some words to it that are meaningful and make sense to you, such as: "I do deserve compassion," "I am seen as valuable and worthy of love," or "I do matter."

   f. Take a snapshot in your mind of this memory and experience to come back to at a later time.

   g. If you'd like, write your experience in your journal. Include what you remembered, what that person said or communicated to you, and how it felt. You will benefit greatly by practicing this exercise daily.

4

The Core of Self-Compassion

Treating Yourself with Kindness

What? Treating ourselves with kindness? This is such a foreign concept. Many of us have been taught to be harsh with ourselves. So what does it mean to treat ourselves with kindness? It is an awareness and a decision to treat oneself as a precious creation of God. It is a choice to be gentle and understanding rather than to treat oneself with harshness and criticism.

It is interesting that most people would agree that we are to be kind, considerate, helpful, and compassionate to others. But somehow, this line of thinking breaks down when we decide how we are supposed to treat ourselves. Most of us would never treat others the way we treat ourselves: in the ways we talk to ourselves, care for ourselves, or help ourselves out when we are in need.

Fortunately, the Bible gives us solid teaching on this when it tells us to love our neighbors as ourselves:

> One of the teachers of the law came and heard them debating. Noticing that Jesus had given them a good answer, he asked him, "Of all the commandments, which is the most important?"
>
> "The most important one," answered Jesus, "is this: 'Hear, O Israel: The Lord our God, the Lord is one. Love the Lord your God with all your heart and with all your soul and with all your mind and with all your strength.' The second is this: 'Love your neighbor as yourself.' There is no commandment greater than these." (Mark 12:28–31)

This is how we love our neighbors:

> Therefore each of you must put off falsehood and speak truthfully to your neighbor, for we are all members of one body. "In your anger do not sin": Do not let the sun go down while you are still angry, and do not give the devil a foothold. Anyone who has been stealing must steal no longer, but must work, doing something useful with their own hands, that they may have something to share with those in need.
>
> Do not let any unwholesome talk come out of your mouths, but only what is helpful for building others up according to their needs, that it may benefit those who listen. And do not grieve the Holy Spirit of God, with whom you were sealed for the day of redemption. Get rid of all bitterness, rage and anger, brawling and slander, along with every form of malice. Be kind and compassionate to one another, forgiving each other, just as in Christ God forgave you. (Eph. 4:25–32)

Based on these two Scriptures, we are to love ourselves in the following ways:

How we speak to ourselves:

In truth, not lies.

Without pent-up anger that causes us to sin.

Building up, not tearing down.

According to what is needed in the moment.

With grace, not with clamor (yelling) and slander.

Ephesians 4:15 says, "Instead, *speaking the truth in love,* we will grow to become in every respect the mature body of him who is the head, that is, Christ" (emphasis added).

How we view ourselves: without bitterness, wrath, anger, and malice.

How we provide for ourselves: working hard so we have something to share with ourselves and others.

How we treat ourselves, especially when we make mistakes or sin: with kindness, tenderheartedness, and forgiveness.

Extending kindness to ourselves means we see ourselves as human beings who are wonderfully made by God and valuable, yet who are imperfect and make mistakes. This plays out in the way we view ourselves, speak to ourselves, listen to ourselves, care for ourselves, and respond to ourselves when we make mistakes.

It also means learning to comfort ourselves and tending to our needs when we are hurt, lonely, tired, disappointed, sad, or angry. This may sound foreign to you because it is such a different way to approach yourself.

When we haven't been taught how to have compassion and kindness for ourselves, it is common to think, *I could never treat myself in such a positive way, I would have no idea how to start, this applies to other people but not me,* or *I could do that in some areas but not this one awful area.*

These conclusions make sense to me in this way: if you have been treated harshly, without kindness and patience, or dismissed and ignored, then kindness and compassion toward yourself will seem very foreign. It is understandable to have a place inside that treats yourself unkindly, like you have already been treated. It is something you may be used to, so in some confusing way it seems right. I'm here to tell you it isn't. One of the keys to even considering kindness toward ourselves involves accepting that it is okay to be human in both having "faults" and in having "strengths."

Learning to Work with Our Failures and Limitations

Sometimes we forget that it is okay to be human. God knows our limitations, and he loves and accepts us completely. We are solidly in the human struggle and will be until the day we die. What I mean is that it is healthy to accept our limitations, tendencies to sin, and imperfections while at the same time pursuing a godly life and character. I think, as Christians, we are tempted to hate or reject aspects of ourselves when we see our negative thoughts, actions, and motivations. This is unhealthy because we get stuck in black-and-white thinking known as *splitting*. We tell ourselves, *I'm nothing, of no value, and worthless because of my sin and imperfection*, or *God completely loves and accepts me and I don't really need to change much about myself because I know God will forgive me*. Both of these stances are unhealthy and will not lead to growth and maturity. We all have to guard against black-and-white thinking that keeps us stuck.

A healthier stance that includes grace and truth sounds like this:

I am a wonderful, priceless person created by God individually. I am also an imperfect person with a sin nature that leads me away from God. God loves and accepts me as his precious child. He wants (and will help) me to become more mature spiritually, intellectually, emotionally, and physically.

God knows that I am human and will succeed and fail in my pursuit of him and maturity. He rejoices in my progress, and

he weeps over the pain and suffering I am going through . . .
some caused by my own actions, and much that results from
living in this imperfect and flawed world, not of my doing. God
is fine with me being human, and I can be too.

This is such a different perspective from the one most of us
have inside. Early abuse, hardships, family stress, and/or neglect cause a separateness to occur within us. We may have
blamed ourselves in some way for the difficulties of childhood,
and thus created an adversarial relationship within us. In fact,
we may have blamed ourselves for something that wasn't our
fault because either we didn't understand the intricacies of what
happened or were inaccurately told something was our fault.

Healing the splits and the adversarial stance inside of us is
sacred work. It involves healing a wound inside that keeps us
stuck in shame and self-blame. When we are kind to ourselves
by responding with both compassion and truth, we work on
healing that split on the inside. We bring together into a supportive whole our two parts: our past self that was too young
to understand the difficulties of childhood experiences, and
the compassion and understanding of a more adult perspective
that can gently calm, soothe, and share the intricacies of what
really went on.

Part of being kind to ourselves includes seeing the multiple
and often complicated layers that occur in most situations rather
than fitting them into a black-and-white way of thinking. I use
a tool with myself and my clients that I call "On the one hand,
on the other hand." This balanced way of relating to ourselves
means we say something like:

On the one hand (whatever the negative is) _____,
   and on the other hand (compassion and understanding
   for self) _____.

I was given the gift of this perspective when I was in the sixth grade. When I was eleven, I played on a softball team, which I loved. I was pretty good at batting and throwing, but terrible at running. My softball coach told me I kept hitting home runs that ended up being triples because I was so slow at running the bases. Oh well . . . can't be good at everything!

One day I was practicing my swing at school during PE. I didn't realize it, but one of my classmates walked behind me as I was practicing my swing. I hit her in the head. She fell to the ground, everyone came over to help her, and the teacher walked her to the nurse's office. I felt horrible! I never meant to hit her. I also didn't check behind me as I was practicing to make sure no one was behind me. I was eleven, and I didn't know any better.

I was crying because I hurt her, and I felt awful. I was also afraid that my classmates and teachers would be mad at me. Right then, one of my friends, Debbie, came up to me and said the most compassionate thing. She put her arm around me and said that she knew I didn't mean to hit my friend, and she felt bad for *me* too. I can't tell you how much that helped. Someone who knew me could see it was an accident, took the time to reach out to me, and let me know she also cared about *my* pain in the situation.

As I look back on that time, here is a truth I could say to myself:

On the one hand, I did swing my bat without looking and hit my classmate in the head. I feel terrible about this. On the other hand, I didn't do it on purpose and will make sure, in the future, that I practice my swing away from others and always look before I swing. I feel terrible about the injury I caused her. I will see how she is doing and sincerely apologize for this unintended injury. I am a nice kid and would not do that on purpose. Everyone makes mistakes, and I am human.

This type of kind response toward myself helped me guard against splitting—that's the tendency to place ourselves in the all-good or all-bad camp. Here are two examples of this type of unhealthy black-and-white thinking:

I hit that girl with my bat, and I'm an awful, terrible person who doesn't care about anyone else.

Yeah, I hit that girl with my bat, but I didn't mean to, and it's not my fault. She shouldn't have been there.

Neither of these options is kind to ourselves. The key is to allow both truths to exist at the same time as we process difficult and painful experiences. We can say to ourselves, *I (made a mistake/ sinned/did something wrong/didn't know everything ahead of time/was immature) and can have compassion for myself as I learn and grow from the situation.*

It is nearly impossible for children to have this kind of balanced thinking. A child's brain is simply not developed enough to see both sides of a situation on their own. Children need a kind adult to explain it to them, because they will naturally think in a black-and-white way and usually end up blaming themselves. This is very important to understand, because so many of the unkind and harsh ways in which we see ourselves now are rooted in childhood conclusions we made about ourselves. These conclusions were often made at a time where our young minds simply didn't have the brain wiring to see a situation clearly and determine that things were much more complicated and multifaceted than they looked.

This reality was made crystal clear to me a number of years ago.

It was a Saturday afternoon. Our daughter was taking a nap, my husband was doing yard work, and I decided to have some one-on-one time with our five-year-old son and make cookies. I got all the ingredients out including the mixer and utensils, while he sat on the other side of the counter ready to help. I asked him to plug the mixer into the outlet next to him. He did exactly as I said . . . as I was putting in the beaters. Big mistake! I had left the mixer in the "on" position, so as he plugged in the mixer my fingers got caught in the spinning beaters. I cried out in pain, unable to pull my fingers out. I yelled at him to unplug the mixer and go get his dad, and he did. He was crying and very distressed, as was I. As my husband helped me remove my fingers from the mixer and tend to my poor bleeding hands, I saw that my little guy had moved to the corner of the room. He was rolled up in a ball and was rocking and saying, "It was my fault, it was my fault," over and over.

I realized what was happening. From his perspective he had caused his mommy to get hurt. He plugged in the mixer, and Mommy got hurt. This was his limited perspective . . . this was all he could see. I picked him up and held him on my lap on the couch. I told him it wasn't his fault, that I had left the mixer on and he hadn't done anything wrong. I told him he was a good boy and he wasn't a problem.

It did no good. He kept crying and insisting it was his fault. My telling him the truth went on for fifteen minutes with no shift in his perspective. I shifted to telling him all the things he did right . . . that he unplugged the mixer when I asked and that he went and got his dad. Still nothing. I then said if it wasn't for him unplugging the mixer and getting his dad, mommy's fingers would have been broken. I saw a shift in his look . . . *Really?* I then saw I had an opening for him to understand. I added that yes, my fingers would have been broken and I would have had to go to the hospital and have casts on my hands. This made a difference. He had been stuck in the pain of knowing that plugging in the mixer caused me to be hurt. Fortunately, when he was provided with this additional information, he was able to shift to how the subsequent actions he had taken helped me to not get hurt more seriously. I milked this new understanding for all it was worth, and it helped him get out of his five-year-old black-and-white thinking.

I am so grateful that I saw him in the corner and heard what he was saying. I'm so grateful that I knew what was happening and came upon words to say that helped him shift out of thinking he was bad and had done something wrong. Even with all those benefits, it took a lot to help him come away with a balanced perspective of what happened.

Most of us did not have the experience of having a parent see what was happening in the moment and then be able to correct our faulty thinking as a child. We were left with our young black-and-white conclusions and no one to explain the truth, or even worse, we were openly blamed for things that weren't our fault. That's why it is so important to do this kind work with ourselves now.

Danny's life with an alcoholic father was full of being blamed for things that he came to learn were not his fault. Danny's dad worked hard all day, came home, and started drinking to ease the stress of the day. As the night wore on his dad would tell Danny and his sisters that he had to drink to deal with his snotty kids. If they were good kids, he wouldn't have to drink. Danny's mom never corrected what his dad said, so he and his sisters believed it was true. They worked harder and harder to be "good" so their dad wouldn't drink, but it never worked. Over the years he drank more and more, no matter how good they were. Finally, as an adult, Danny realized he was still trying to please his dad, even though he had died years ago.

Danny joined an Al-Anon group years ago to help him deal with a lifetime of codependency and trying to please those in his life. He began to learn that his dad's drinking was his dad's responsibility, and that he was always a good enough kid. He began practicing compassion toward himself, and while it felt life-giving in one way, it was also uncomfortable at times because he was so used to blaming himself and trying harder to be good enough.

He is now saying things to himself such as:

My dad's drinking was his way of coping with and numbing his pain. I was a good son who did a lot of things right and made normal mistakes. I deserved to have a dad who wasn't an alcoholic and a mom who was present for me. I did the best I could do raising myself emotionally. I am learning to validate and encourage myself as well as learning ways to cope with pain and stress that don't hurt me or someone else. It's okay for me to be in the process of growing. When I feel the old feelings of not being good enough, I will take some deep breaths and remind myself that I am good enough and that I have friends, God, and myself to connect with now. I don't have to do things perfectly, and I'm not alone in this.

Learning to Work with Our Talents and Gifts

Another way of being kind to ourselves includes discovering, embracing, and exercising the gifts and talents God has given us. Part of being human is finding a balanced way of accepting that God has a plan for each of us to positively impact others for him. I often hear others completely discount the ways they bless others, saying things such as, "I could have never done this without God," or "I had nothing to do with it, it was God." I know I'm probably ruffling some feathers right now . . . hang in there. I believe completely that God's grace gives us specific gifts and abilities. We can be 100 percent grateful to him and praise him for that. It is also true that we are to be obedient to his leading and gifting and be active in exercising those gifts.

I think of Billy Graham as an example. There is no doubt that he has an extraordinary gift of leading others to Christ. This is a gift bestowed upon him by God. At the same time, Billy Graham has been obedient to God for seventy years in his endless study of the Scriptures, his relationship with God, and a life of traveling that included stress on him and his family. Yes, God is to be 100 percent praised for Graham's gift and anointing, and at the same time Dr. Graham can be pleased and grateful that when he gets to heaven God will say, "Well done, good and faithful servant."

Here's a balanced way to speak to yourself about the positive impact you've made on your children, spouse, friends, coworkers, neighbors, those in need, or others you have influence over:

> God made me who I am, with specific interests, talents, and passions. He wants me to impact others with his love and care, and he has equipped me specifically to do so. He and I are a team. He has given me these gifts and desires to do good works in specific ways, and it is up to me to take action as he leads me. It is healthy to rejoice in how God uses me in a specific moment to bless another while at the same time giving him the glory for equipping me in this way. It feels good to me when I've been a blessing to another. Isn't it like God to bless me while using me to bless someone else? Thanks, God!

I wonder if our discomfort in accepting a compliment for how God uses us comes more from a lack of compliments as a child or from never being taught how to accept them. Believe it or not, we don't instinctively know how to accept a compliment.

Here's a story in my life where I learned this firsthand: our daughter was about four, and I gave her a compliment about what a nice job she was doing coloring. For the first time, she looked embarrassed and seemed like she didn't know what to say. Before this, if I encouraged or complimented her, she would get a big smile and take it in. I realized that developmentally she was becoming more aware of herself and was trying to figure out what to do with this compliment coming her way. I asked her, "Do you not know what to do?" She shook her head. "No." I said, "Oh, I gave you a compliment, telling you something I liked about you. When someone says something nice about you,

you can tell yourself, 'I am a very nice girl and very wonderful,' and then tell the other person, 'Thank you.'"

She smiled, and I suggested we try that again. "You are a very good artist. I love the way you are coloring," I said. She paused and then said, "I am a very nice girl and am good at coloring. Thank you." And, amazingly, she seemed to be able to accept compliments after that.

We are exactly the same way. We all need to be taught how to receive a compliment for how we blessed another and/or how we are good at something. For some this will be relatively easy, and for others it will be very difficult. That's okay. What matters is not where you start but that there is gradual movement. I'm always amazed and grateful when someone shares with me how the words I've spoken during counseling, speaking, or in my writing have had a positive impact on them. I usually respond with how glad I am that what I said was a blessing, and how grateful I am that God let me have the opportunity.

I am also incredibly grateful for the ways in which God uses others in my life to bless and care for me. I finished treatment for breast cancer in April 2014 after a very difficult ten months of surgery, chemotherapy, and radiation. God was with me throughout, and I praise him for this in ways I cannot put into words. He took care of me through my relationship with him and also by raising an army of people to support me through it.

Each one of those who reached out made an impact on me and held me up. It helped me not feel so alone through such a difficult process. I tear up as I write this . . . so many people responded to God's urging to bless me during such a difficult time. I don't know how I could have gotten through it without all of them. What if they had ignored God's urging?

It's okay to be human and use the gifts God has given you to bless others. It's okay to be glad that God used you in the life of another. It's okay to acknowledge this while praising God at the same time. God is delighted when you are being a blessing to someone else, and you can rejoice in how he blessed others through you too.

Kindness through the Fruits of the Spirit

Galatians 5:22–23 is another passage that can inspire us to treat ourselves in a biblically sound way:

> But the fruit of the Spirit is love, joy, peace, forbearance, kindness, goodness, faithfulness, gentleness and self-control. Against such things there is no law.

These verses describe characteristics that emanate from someone who is yielded to the Holy Spirit. When we are in tune with him and connected to him, we naturally experience and express these characteristics toward everyone—including ourselves.

Love	Joy	Peace	Forbearance	Kindness
Goodness	Faithfulness	Gentleness	Self-Control

Imagine what it would be like if you interacted with yourself in the above ways . . . it would make a world of difference.

You and I were each created by God as a precious, valuable person, and we deserve kindness, care, empathy, understanding, and comfort. This is how God feels toward us, and this is how he wants us to learn to interact with ourselves. It grieves him to see us carrying the pain and lies from mistreatment by others who were hurt and damaged themselves and who passed that on to us.

The wonderful news is that this kind and compassionate way of responding to ourselves is truly possible. You could be the one who comes alongside yourself with empathy and says, *Yes, it would be so hard to:*

Be heartbroken.

Have your life turn out so differently than you thought.

Lose your job.

Be devastatingly hurt by someone you trusted.

Have conflict with your children, parents, friends, or spouse.

Not be in the relationship you desire.

Not be able to have children.

Be in a job that is harmful and/or unsatisfying.

Be betrayed.

Grow up in a family in which you feel dismissed, hurt, or lost.

Be single when you want to be married.

Be in a dysfunctional relationship that you don't think you can survive without.

Be stuck in an addiction.

Not feel close to God anymore.

What other type of compassionate statements would you like to hear from yourself? *Yes, it would be so hard to . . .*

You could also be the one who comes alongside yourself with encouragement and says:

I'm proud of myself; I worked so hard for that.

I am a kind and compassionate person.

I have shown such strength, perseverance, and courage in all I have been through.

I matter, and what I need matters.

I matter to God, and he desperately loves me.

I have good character in the way I interact with people.

I have important gifts God has given me, and I am using them.

I am working so hard on growing and learning as a person, and it shows.

I am a valuable person, no matter what.

This is a wonderful accomplishment. I should soak it in.

What other type of encouraging statements would you like to hear from yourself? As you ponder all that has been shared about being kind to yourself, here is something you might say to yourself right now:

> This is all so new. To think that I was created to be treated with kindness, understanding, empathy, care, and comfort seems too good to be true. To think that God sees me this way is both wonderful and a little hard to believe at the same time. It honestly seems so unbelievable to think I could learn to treat myself in this way. I don't even know where to start. I'm willing to give it a try. I am taking a step in reading this book, and that's a good start. I am cautiously optimistic and will give this a try a little bit at a time.

Concluding Reflections

As we come to the close of this chapter, take a moment to check in with yourself about how you are doing. If you would like, ponder the questions below to help process what you've read:

1. What is it like to realize that the Bible encourages us to love ourselves?
2. In what ways would you like to be more kind to yourself?
   ___ The way I speak to myself.
   ___ Comforting myself when distressed.
   ___ Allowing myself to be human.
   ___ Taking better care of myself.
   ___ Giving myself grace when I make mistakes.
   ___ Accepting my strengths.
   ___ Encouraging myself.
   ___ Being my own best friend.
   ___ Being gentle with myself.

3. What would the days, weeks, and months ahead look like if you practiced more kindness toward yourself?

4. Whose story did you most relate to in this chapter? What type of new thoughts or feelings of compassion were you able to have for that person? How might these new ways of understanding apply to you as well?

5. Try a moment of kindness toward yourself:

   a. Gently place your hand comfortably over your heart.

   b. Take a few gentle breaths as you welcome a moment of calm into your life.

   c. Notice this kind connection with yourself, and say some words that are soothing to you, such as: "I can learn to be kind to myself. It is okay for me to be human with faults and strengths. God sees me with kindness and compassion, and I can too."

   d. Repeat this gentle action daily as you build this kindness and compassion with yourself one moment at a time.

5

How Self-Compassion
Helps All of Our Relationships

Praise be to the God and Father of our Lord Jesus Christ,
the Father of compassion and the God of all comfort,
who comforts us in all our troubles, so that we can comfort those in any trouble with the comfort we ourselves
receive from God.

2 Corinthians 1:3–4

As we take in God's comfort, we are able to extend that
comfort to others. In my own life I've also noticed that
as I extend compassion to myself, I am able to more
easily extend it to others.

John had always been a stickler for doing things "right." His
dad had taught him that there was a right way and a wrong
way to do things, and nothing existed in between. John did not
receive a lot of compassion and understanding growing up, and
he had learned to live without it. John was grateful that his dad
had taught him a lot of skills for living life. These skills made it

easier for him to succeed in school and eventually in his career, and he reaped the benefits of these disciplines in his life. The problem was that John didn't seem to know how to handle things that didn't work out, and he especially couldn't tolerate it when his wife and kids messed up. His family wanted him to care about their feelings and be patient when they made mistakes. His wife told him on many occasions that it was normal for kids to mess up and that they learned things in steps. She wanted their home to be one in which all of them could fail and still be fully accepted. For a part of himself, this felt like "nails on a chalkboard." Another part of him thought it sounded nice . . . like a way he would have liked to be treated growing up.

His inability to have compassion for his family's human foibles caused problems. His children and wife began distancing themselves from him and sharing less and less about their lives with him. John loved his family deeply and wanted to be close to them. He felt like he was supposed to relate in a way that he was ill-equipped to, even though he wanted to. He was at a loss for what to do. One thing he did know was that pushing for perfection and showing a lack of compassion were not working.

John was a good man who loved his family but he lacked the ability to accept "humanness" in himself and others and to relate in compassionate, accepting ways. There was great hope for John because he loved his family, and he was willing to admit that the way he was relating wasn't working. That was wonderful progress and would help him to take some important next steps:

- Being willing to find out why compassion was so hard for him.
- Working through the pain that was still lodged inside about the harsh way he was raised emotionally and how he was unintentionally passing that on to his family.
- Gently learning and practicing ways to be compassionate with himself.

- Naturally passing on this new perspective and way of relating with his family.

What John discovered, and the rest of us will, is that developing a compassionate relationship with yourself doesn't just benefit you. In fact, it will benefit all of your relationships.

Compassion for Others

When we have compassion for ourselves, we more easily show compassion to others. Conversely, when we have a judgmental attitude toward ourselves, we tend to be judgmental toward others, especially if they struggle in the same areas we judge ourselves in. Therefore, as we learn to see and treat ourselves with compassion, all of our relationships will benefit.

As John worked with himself in therapy, he came to find that he suffered greatly as a child by having to be so perfect to please his father and avoid his anger. He had to wall off any compassion for himself or others in order to survive emotionally. The wonderful news was that over time he was able to have compassion for what he went through as a little guy. As he began to interact with himself in more understanding ways, he noticed that he was naturally more compassionate toward his wife and children. This transformation happened over time, and the harsh part of him would sneak back in here and there. Perfection wasn't the goal . . . movement in a compassionate direction was. It took some time for his wife and kids to begin to trust him, and very slowly they began to open up to him. No one did all this perfectly, nor did they need to.

Better Friends, Parents, Spouses, and Coworkers

This is what the LORD Almighty said: "Administer true justice; show mercy and compassion to one another." (Zech. 7:9)

When we are in better emotional health and are a compassionate best friend to ourselves, we are more balanced and effective in all of our relationships. This makes sense. When we are more content on the inside we are easier to deal with, more good-natured, more even-keeled, and less easily triggered emotionally. When we feel more settled on the inside, we are less vulnerable and do not need other people to respond the exact way we need in order to feel okay.

When we can soak in the positives and negatives of who we are, as well as soak in God's love and acceptance, it gives us confidence and an experience of being settled inside. If we are accepting of the areas in which we are still growing, someone commenting on them won't hurt to the core, and we won't become defensive or aggressive in response.

Emily was in the next room while her kids were playing with their friends. One of her son's friends was complaining about how his mom did yoga in the middle of the living room every night and interfered with his ability to play his new video game. Emily's son, Darin, piped up without hesitation, saying that he'd never have to worry about that because his mom never exercised. That comment pierced Emily's heart, and she stomped out and scolded Darin in front of his friends. "You take that back, what a mean thing to say about your mother. If I don't exercise it is because I'm always taking care of you kids." She then made Darin apologize, and then she went back into the other room. In part, she felt good for making him take back such mean words about her, but part of her also felt awful. Somewhere inside she knew he didn't deserve all that. Shortly thereafter the friends went home, and she noticed Darin went up to his room with a dejected look on his face.

Emily did a courageous thing by stopping to ask herself where all that anger had come from. As she prayed and sought God's wisdom, she became aware the anger was actually toward herself. The reality was that Darin was right; she didn't exercise. All he had done was tell the truth, and not in a mean way. Her own disgust with herself for not taking care of herself physically had been hurled at Darin. She felt awful once she realized it and cried at the injury she had caused him. Not only had she scolded him for simply stating the truth but she had also blamed him and his brother for her lack of exercise.

After calming down a little, she knocked on Darin's door and asked if she could come in. He reluctantly agreed. She apologized to him by saying, "I am so sorry that I yelled at you in front of your friends. I should never have done that. There is nothing wrong with what you said. You were just stating the truth. I don't exercise, and I was wrong in saying I didn't because of taking care of you and your brother. The truth is I don't exercise because I don't make the time to do it, and I don't even know where to start. I feel angry and ashamed about this, and all that anger toward myself came out all over you. I am so sorry. You did nothing wrong. I'm going to work on myself to try to make sure I don't do that to you again. I'd be happy to apologize to your friends if you'd like me to. Will you forgive me?"

Darin was shocked. He had never heard his mom apologize like this. He stood up and hugged her, and he forgave her.

Emily gave him a great gift that day. She owned her own misbehavior, repaired her relationship with Darin, and more importantly gave him an experience of how to do the same in his own life and relationships in the future. Emily also gave herself a great gift. She not only owned her misbehavior but also decided to try to understand it; in addition, she began honestly looking at why she wasn't caring for herself in the ways she wanted. This move toward understanding herself on the inside created a new path for her in which she could grow and express compassion toward herself.

Responsibility for Our Well-Being

One way we make others responsible for our well-being is to ignore our own instincts in a situation and instead defer to another person. We aren't deferring out of kindness; we do it out of mistrusting the instincts God has given us or out of fear of speaking up. Furthermore, we often end up blaming the other person for not considering us in the decision. In reality, we may not have shared our opinion on the issue or how important it was to us. Advocating for yourself, regardless of the result, is a very compassionate and connecting thing to do for yourself. When you give your well-being over to the opinions and actions of others, it often doesn't work out for you *or* the other person.

Another way we make others responsible for our well-being is by not caring for ourselves. Some resist caring for themselves because they feel they are being selfish. The converse is actually true: when we don't care for ourselves compassionately, we place more responsibility on others to make things okay for us emotionally. When we harshly judge ourselves for normal human weaknesses, we often look to others to say that these shortcomings are "no big deal" so we don't have to feel the pain inside. This causes others to craft their responses so as to not "set us off," make us sad, or leave us feeling anxious.

Here's an example. Let's say I'm down on myself for not doing a good job at something, and I need reassurance. This is a normal need. If I haven't developed the skills to take a compassionate stance toward myself, I will look *solely* toward others to meet this need. It is not unhealthy to ask for reassurance, but *the habit of looking to others for external validation becomes unbalanced if the sole source of my well-being lies in how someone else responds to my situation.*

When this happens, we often have all kinds of high expectations of others and become quite self-focused about how they need to respond to us. Taking a compassionate stance toward ourselves helps us to soothe our distress before we become totally invested in another person's response.

When our kids were in grade school, I noticed that when I would do extra-nice things for them I would expect them to be extra-grateful for what a "wonderful" mom I was. I had grown up that way myself—needing to overly thank and affirm my mom so she would feel good about herself. It was hard on me to know my response was going to determine my mom's well-being, especially when she seemed to respond differently each time.

Once I realized that I was repeating this unwritten expectation with my own kids, forcing them to effusively thank me for the little extras I would do for them, I decided I needed to change my expectation and responses. I did not want them to grow up having to ponder and strategize how to meet my needs. So I changed a few things. For starters, I pulled back from doing some extra things for a while, during the time I worked it through, because I knew I hadn't grown enough to respond appropriately.

I worked on it in therapy and got in touch with how hard it had been for me as a kid to respond positively without fail in order to meet my mother's needs for frequent affirmation. As I processed a lot of my feelings, it helped drain some of the pressure I felt that I had then been projecting onto my kids. I also started to talk to myself before I did anything extra for the kids:

> How will I feel if they just say a nice "thank you" but aren't as excited as I am? I want them to be kids and not have to meet my needs. I'm not going to expect them to be older and more responsive than they are. I'm only going to do this if it is a "no-strings-attached" gift to them.

This helped a lot because I didn't speak to myself in a self-condemning way—it was more of a "coming alongside as a kind big sister" way. Over several months, these things helped me not have those responses anymore. I was able to have compassion for myself as I saw that I was unconsciously repeating a pattern with my kids that I had experienced myself. It didn't make me or my mom bad (she probably had the same thing done to her), it just made me aware. Out of love for my kids and a desire to be the best imperfect mom I could be, I worked on the core of unresolved pain that was causing me to repeat this pattern with my children.

Protection against Depression and Anxiety

One of the most encouraging results of research on the benefits of self-compassion shows that those who are more self-compassionate also tend to have less anxiety and depression.[1] This makes so much sense. When our shortcomings and mistakes are met with compassion and understanding, we will have more energy and space inside to forgive ourselves and find solutions. When our shortcomings and mistakes are met with self-judgment and condemnation, we experience a lack of hope and begin to shut down emotionally. We may experience depression and anxiety as we try to either never make a mistake or anticipate every awful thing that *may* happen.

One of the things inherent to depression and anxiety is the tendency to ruminate on depressive and anxious thoughts. We don't do this because we want to think in unhealthy ways. Rather, we do this as a way to try to work things through and come to a better place. The problem is that if you only know to think about what you *should* have done, or what awful thing *might* happen, you end up thinking in a circular way with no resolution.

Self-compassion offers new truthful information that can help break this rumination cycle. For starters, it is very important if you struggle with anxiety and depression that you do not judge yourself for this. Anxiety and depression are not the same, but they often occur together. Part of extending compassion to yourself is coming to an understanding that there are many factors involved in whether or not a person develops depression and/or anxiety. Some of these factors include:

Your Natural Brain Wiring

From birth, babies come out of the womb with varying levels of anxiety and the ability to be soothed and comforted. You may be someone who was born with a tendency to be high-strung, but that doesn't mean you are doomed to be anxious or depressed. It does mean you deserve compassion and understanding if these are tendencies for you. This book provides tools to care for yourself in ways that help you with these leanings.

Family History

Some people who struggle with anxiety and depression also have family members who have struggled in similar ways, often for generations. Whether this occurs through a genetic predisposition or through the effects of being raised by those who struggled with depression or anxiety is not known for sure. What you can take away from this is compassion for yourself if these have been factors in your life.

Life Experiences

A history of difficult life experiences can definitely impact a person's ability to ward off depression and anxiety, especially if a person struggles with symptoms of post-traumatic stress. (We'll explore this in more detail in chapter nine.) PTSD is a far more common occurrence than most people realize, and there is great hope for people finding help and relief with the proper treatment. If this applies to you, allow yourself some compassion for the toll this has taken on you. There is hope that you can learn ways that will help soothe your system and care for yourself.

Physical Health Problems

Ongoing physical problems may trigger anxiety and depression. Some of these may include hormonal or thyroid problems, diabetes, heart disease, asthma, and side effects of medical treatments or prescriptions. If you have a concern about any of these or other medical conditions you are dealing with, contact your doctor for an evaluation.

Substance Use

Heavy or long-term use of substances such as alcohol, cannabis, amphetamines, sedatives, or other drugs can cause people to develop or worsen anxiety and depression.

Everyone is different, and it is often a combination of factors that contributes to a person developing depression and/or anxiety. If you struggle in these ways, seek evaluation and treatment from a mental health professional. The wonderful news is that self-compassion can help ward off these conditions as well as reduce their effects. The healthy way to use the information above is to talk to yourself with compassion about what you've learned.

> Reading the list of the many factors that contribute to depression and anxiety impacted me. In one way it was hard, but in another way it gives me a bit of compassion for myself. As I was reading, I heard a part of me say, "Well, no wonder it's been so hard; no wonder I've struggled; see, this isn't all my fault." I'm realizing that there are valid reasons why I've struggled with depression and anxiety for so long. It makes sense that my system may not have come into this world fully functioning, and some of the tough things I've been dealing with have really depleted me and worn me down. This makes so much sense . . . I can actually feel a little relief inside and feel compassion for myself for going through this for so long. It also gives me hope that as I learn to extend myself kindness, compassion, and self-care, I will feel calmer and less distressed. I want to feel better and get the help I need.

Teaching and Modeling Self-Compassion

We can't teach what we don't practice ourselves. When compassionate responses are a part of us, they will flow out of us in the ways we respond to ourselves and in the ways we respond to others. Lessons about how to be self-compassionate are mainly caught, not taught. This means that when others see this demonstrated naturally in everyday life, they will learn it naturally and it will become a part of them too. One of the best things you can do for those you are in relationship with is to develop compassion for yourself.

Mona sat down on the couch in amazement at what just happened. A few moments ago, her eight-year-old daughter, Anne, came to her crying about how she could never finish doing her math homework. She felt stupid and defeated. Normally Mona would give her either a stern lecture or a pep talk . . . both of which communicated that she should ignore her feelings and do it anyway. This time though, Mona felt compassion for her daughter and could understand how, after a long day at school and soccer practice, Anne would be worn out and feeling unable to do math.

Mona pulled Anne up into her lap and let her cry. She told Anne that she loved her and that she thought maybe she was tired and worn out . . . this made so much sense after a long, active day. Mona told Anne she could stay there and snuggle as long as she wanted, and when she was filled up inside she could give her homework another try. Mona assured her she would be happy to help her figure it out if she needed help. She marveled at how Anne calmed down inside; after a short while, she did her homework with only a little help here and there.

Mona was also surprised at how this response came from inside herself. Maybe all the work she was doing to be compassionate to herself was now helping her daughter too.

Repair Relational Missteps

The ability to be more compassionate toward ourselves for mistakes we make or hurts we cause enables us to own and repair them. In chapter 2, we learned that a lack of compassion can lead to either narcissism or self-contempt. This happens when we are unable to healthily acknowledge an error we've made. When this happens, we tend to either collapse under shame or defend ourselves against acknowledging any responsibility for the situation at all. Both of these patterns take the focus off of repairing the relationship with the other person or righting the wrong.

In contrast, when we have self-compassion and "mess up," we don't need to beat ourselves up. We can acknowledge that we made a mistake, sinned, or did something that wasn't ideal. We can then go back to the person or situation and not only take steps to repair the damage we caused but also establish a reconnection with that person.

You can say to yourself, *I made a mistake. I'd like to go back and make this better.* We don't have to make ourselves all bad (shame) or the other person all bad (blame). We can speak to ourselves with a balance of grace and truth: *I really goofed up there. I can go back and repair the mistake I made. I'm a valuable person who made a mistake in this situation.*

Developing a compassionate relationship with yourself promotes healthy relationships with everyone in your life—including you! Here's something compassionate you might say to yourself about this new idea:

> Wow, I didn't realize that building a compassionate relationship with myself will also benefit all my relationships. I sure wish I'd known this before. The good news is it isn't too late. I'm not quite sure how to start, but I'm willing to learn. I like the idea that as I'm learning to develop this new, kinder relationship with myself, it will spread to others.

Concluding Reflections

As we come to the close of this chapter, take a moment to check in with yourself about how you are doing. If you would like, ponder the questions below to help process what you've read:

1. What was it like to realize that building a compassionate relationship with yourself would actually benefit *all* of your relationships?

2. How has what you've learned affected your desire to build a compassionate relationship with yourself?

3. What traits or shortcomings are you judgmental of in yourself that you also have trouble tolerating in others? Who will you have an easier time being compassionate with as you take in more compassion for yourself?

4. What steps do you want to take to increase compassion for yourself? Check those that apply.

   ____ Acknowledging that things aren't working in a certain area of your life.

   ____ Being willing to explore why compassion is so hard for you through journaling or talking with a trusted friend.

   ____ Working through the pain that is still lodged inside that is accidentally spilling onto your family and friends now. Possible ways to work on this are journaling, entering into therapy, joining a support group, or sharing with a trusted friend.

   ____ Gently learning and practicing ways to be compassionate with yourself.

5. Try a compassion moment I call "Soaking in the Compassion a Good Friend Would Have for You." (If it is difficult to come up with a good friend who might respond to you in

this way, you can use someone you admire who is compassionate or use a fictional character you really relate to. It could be someone in a book or movie or a past historical character whom you know you could experience a compassionate response from.)

- Get comfortable and relaxed, and imagine that you are sitting down with a good friend and telling them about a difficult situation in your life that is occurring right now.
- Notice how they might look at you and respond to you as you tell your story. Notice the compassion in your friend's eyes and the empathy on their face. Notice what it feels like to have someone understand you and connect with you in this way.
- Allow yourself to soak that compassion in at an even deeper level. Breathe it in through your whole body.
- Allow a little of that compassion to come from you to yourself as well. Breathe it in through your whole body.
- Attach some words to it that are meaningful and make sense to you, such as: *I am going through a tough time. My friend sees me as valuable and deserving of compassion. I do matter.*
- Take a snapshot in your mind of this memory and experience to come back to at a later time.

If you'd like, write your experience in your journal. Include what you remembered, what that person said or communicated to you, and how it felt to take that in.

6

A Compassionate View
of Self-Care

Suzanne was attending a women's brunch in hopes of making some friends at the new church she had started to attend. The speaker kept talking about how important it was to "do self-care." Suzanne was irritated . . . this wasn't helping. First of all, she didn't even know what the woman was talking about. What did she mean, self-care? Suzanne did take care of herself. She ate healthy (most of the time), got enough sleep (some of the time), and had a place to live and clothes to wear. What was the speaker talking about? *Isn't self-care just spoiling yourself and being selfish?* she thought. But as the speaker kept sharing, Suzanne's eyes were opened to a whole new way of looking at herself and caring for herself in a way that was balanced and healthy.

I was that speaker, and here are some of the truths I shared at that women's brunch: I believe self-care is important, and I believe it is biblical. I believe it is vital for a healthy, balanced life even though it is unnatural and difficult for most people. If you are nodding right now, you are in the majority, just like Suzanne.

Why is this? There are a lot of reasons. It is very important to understand why this happens, because it will help you develop compassion rather than contempt for yourself and your struggles in this area. Ideally, learning to care for oneself develops naturally when we are cared for, valued, and shown specific ways to care for our body, mind, emotions, and spirit. When raised in this kind of supportive environment, the desire to care for oneself and the skills to do so develop naturally. However, when we haven't been shown how to care for all the aspects of ourselves, these skills don't develop. The good news is it isn't too late to learn.

So, what gets in the way of self-care developing naturally? The following list is not meant to put down those who raised us. They most likely did the best they could with what they knew. It's hard to pass on healthy self-care practices if you've never learned them yourself. Regardless, even when the lack is not intended, missing certain aspects of our development has an effect on our ability to care for ourselves.

The Six Areas of Self-Care

Developing children need to be shown how to do everything. If neglect occurs, and we don't receive instruction, skills, and encouragement to practice the following areas of self-care, we won't know how to do them instinctually.

Physical. We all need instruction and modeling in the areas of hygiene, good nutrition, and exercise. If we did not receive what we needed in this area, it will be hard to care for ourselves in these ways, even if as an adult we know it is important.

Emotional. First, children need to get filled up emotionally through time with loved ones, attention, play, empathy, and physical affection. Children may show the effects of an unmet need in this area by a vacant look in their eyes, distancing themselves from others, an insatiable need for attention, or out of control behavior due to lack of discipline. Second, children need to be taught how to regulate their emotions. Learning how to name and value their emotions, as well as how to work through these emotions without being ruled by them, will benefit them their whole lives. Most people don't know how to do this. If we didn't learn these skills as we were growing up, this will be an area of struggle. (Chapters 7, 8, and 9 give lots of help in this area.)

Educational. Every child loves to learn. If we were not read to, given help with homework, shown study skills, or challenged academically, we may have trouble caring for our intellectual self. This will be especially true if we had an undiagnosed and untreated learning disability.

Social. We are relational beings and need social connection with others. This need may not be met if a child does not experience normal social interactions with family members, peers, and other adults. Children may grow up not knowing how to interact with others in socially acceptable ways. This may impair their friendships as well as their relationships as adults.

Spiritual. The Bible tells us that every human being sees evidence of God all around us through his creation:

For since the creation of the world God's invisible qualities—his eternal power and divine nature—have been clearly seen, being understood from what has been made, so that people are without excuse. (Rom. 1:20)

It is a normal, healthy instinct to seek to know the One who created us. If we were not given healthy spiritual experiences and instruction, we most likely missed learning about God and ways to be close to him. Conversely, if we were given a view of God as distant, controlling, legalistic, or harsh, we will feel very mixed or even negative toward him. In addition, if our parents were overly involved at church we may come to resent church and God. Children instinctually know that love is spelled T-I-M-E. If children see their parents excessively pouring their time and energy into church and others, they could feel neglected and unimportant. The pain they feel may then become transferred onto church and God. Many parents did not have healthy spiritual training themselves and so were not able to share it with their children. I take comfort in knowing that God loves each one he has created and will pursue a personal and healing relationship with them.

Medical. Children experience medical neglect when they are not provided with adequate medical, dental, or mental health care, including regular checkups, preventative care, and treatment of illnesses. This lack of care can have lasting results and affects physical and emotional health.

When Needs Go Unmet

Life is hard, and sometimes families are doing the best they can just to survive. When this happens, children's emotional and relational needs often suffer. This means their needs for emotional and physical connection, playtime with parents, and emotionally connected relationships with family members may go unmet.

Although the deprivation may have been unintentional, a person who did not get these needs met will often feel "less than," not important, not valuable, or not worthy. If we did not get time, attention, and care as children, this can translate into feeling as adults that we are not worthy of being cared for. We often treat ourselves with the same level of care that we were given, which may not have been enough.

We Over-Focus on Others

Many times we can get in a habit of focusing on others to an unhealthy degree. This can happen due to a need to please others and avoid rejection or anger. It can also happen through a long-term habit of being the strong one who cared for others as we grew up. When a person has grown up this way, they develop a special sensitivity to the needs of others because they know what it is like to have a need that isn't being met. They are often drawn to meet the needs of others as a vicarious way of meeting their own unmet needs, and are often not even aware they are doing this. While caring for others is a noble effort, it can be harmful to us if our focus does not include caring for ourselves as well.

Joanne loved her new church. Everyone was so friendly and cared so much about those in the community. There were lots of opportunities to volunteer, and she dove right in. She started with helping in the church's food closet as well as providing child care for single moms in the neighborhood who needed a break. She knew what it felt like to grow up struggling and having to handle everything on her own. It felt so good to help those in need and know she was really making a difference. Pretty soon Joanne also started volunteering with the women's ministry as well as heading up the team welcoming new visitors. Everyone was so grateful to her for her help, it was almost addicting. But even though things were going great at church, they were not going so well at home. Joanne's high school–age kids felt like they never saw her, her house was a mess, she rarely ever spent time with her friends, and she had stopped working out.

Joanne's need for approval and affirmation caused her to be out of balance in the rest of her life, and it was beginning to affect her health, home, family, and friendships in negative ways.

Joanne didn't know it, but she was being so helpful both as a way to soothe the pain she carried inside, from growing up without the help she needed, as well as a way to feel worthy and valuable by being appreciated. Joanne was willing to listen to feedback from various sources about how out of balance her life had become. She began to talk to herself with compassion about the problems that were resulting from her good intentions:

> I think it is a blessing that I am able to recognize those in need and help. I know I am making a difference to a lot of people who really need it. I know it would have made a huge difference to me when I was young if someone had recognized what I needed and stepped in to help meet my needs. I also realize that without meaning to I have neglected my health, kids, home, and friends. I truly care about all these areas too. Rather than drop my volunteering, I will ask my friend Susie to help me come up with a plan to make sure my own needs of exercise and rest are met, as well as take time for my kids, home, and friends. It won't be easy to reduce some of the areas of service that bring me so many accolades. I think I need to spend some time encouraging and connecting to myself, rather than seeking all of that from other people.

We Stay in Stressful Environments

Life is stressful . . . there is no doubt about it. There are ways to reduce the amount of stress we experience as well as ways to cope with and manage stress, but there is no way to completely avoid it. Staying in chronically stressful environments causes us to operate in survival mode, which usually trumps any self-care we had planned. The good news is that there are ways to take breaks from stressful situations as well as skills we can practice to manage our stress more effectively (see chapters 8 and 9).

We Stop Caring for Ourselves

Even when we have been raised in a supportive, loving environment, the circumstances of life can hit, and we may stop caring for ourselves. If this applies to you, ask yourself, *When did I stop caring about myself?* More often than not this occurs because of one of three reasons:

Abuse as a child (emotional/verbal, physical, sexual, spiritual). When this occurs, great damage is done to a person's self-esteem and view of himself or herself as valuable and worthy of care. Abuse treats a person like an object, and the victim ends up feeling like one. You lose some of your personhood, power, and worth as you are used by another person to meet their own needs. As a recipient of their anger, frustration, and control, you become disconnected from your needs, and this makes it hard to care for yourself, even as an adult.

Neglect as a child. Unlike abuse, neglect is usually typified by an ongoing pattern of inadequate care and is often observed by others, such as teachers, once a child starts to attend school. Neglect is usually seen in the six previously described areas: physical, emotional, educational, social, spiritual, and medical. Neglect is damaging because it gives the child the message that they are invisible, not valuable, and not worth taking care of. This damaging message then gets internalized, and as adults we end up treating ourselves in the same way.

Involvement in an abusive relationship as an adult (emotional/verbal, physical, sexual, spiritual). Staying in a harmful relationship can cause our self-esteem to plummet, and this can result in stopping care of oneself. This can happen in a close personal relationship, work relationship, or close friendship. We can stay in these relationships for a variety of reasons.

- Sometimes we stay because of deep-seated feelings of abandonment from childhood that cause us to put up with anything to avoid being alone.

- We became so harmed in this relationship that we find it difficult to get out either because we do not have resources to make it alone or because we've been brainwashed into believing we don't deserve anything better and can't make it alone.

- We want to honor our marital vows, even if being abused has systematically broken us down on the inside. The desire to keep our vows is honorable and godly, but allowing a relationship to remain abusive is not taking care of ourselves the way God intended. Seeking a structured separation while the abuse is addressed is often a healthy way to respond. This approach addresses the abusive patterns, as well as the damage being done to the spouse and children. I am always shocked and dismayed by how often I see a spouse being encouraged to "hang in there" in an abusive living situation while the abuser is not held accountable.

- We stay in an emotionally abusive job or friendship because we are used to be spoken to or treated in demeaning ways. It isn't that we like being treated this way, but it is what we are used to. Because of this, we may not realize that we don't deserve to be treated this way, don't have to tough it out, and can find another job or friends who are respectful to us.

This short overview describes understandable reasons why we may not automatically think of ways to care for ourselves or know how to. Use what you responded to in this section to understand yourself better, and practice speaking to yourself with compassion about this. Here's a way you might talk to yourself:

> I didn't realize how many reasons there are to explain why I never learned to care for myself or why I may have stopped caring along the way. I feel sad and angry that so much time has been lost. I realize I'm not a bad person for not knowing some things other people seem to just know. I'm going to treat myself with compassion over what I've missed rather than beat myself up for something I didn't cause. At the same time, it is my job to care for myself now. I can be proud of myself for beginning this journey to develop a compassionate relationship with myself. I can learn a little at a time and see what works for me. It's not too late. I've already started the process.

Assessing Your Self-Care Needs

Self-care is essentially listening to and responding to your needs in healthy ways. There is a difference between being selfish and practicing self-care. Being selfish means you are only considering your needs without considering the needs of others. Self-care is being a steward of yourself and your God-given needs while also being aware of the needs of others. Notice your response to the idea that self-care involves listening to and responding to your needs in healthy ways. What is your gut reaction? People generally have some different reactions to this:

What needs? I don't have needs.

I'm not supposed to have needs.

I don't have time to have needs . . . I'm taking care of everyone else!

I don't even know what my needs are; I don't know where to start.

I have needs, but there is no one to meet them, so what's the point?

I have needs, but I feel guilty even having them.

I have needs, but I don't know how to share them.

If I think about my needs it will make it hard for me to think about what other people need.

Our needs are created by God and help us keep in touch with where we are fulfilled and what areas need attention. Remember, you are just learning self-care. Celebrate the healthy things you are doing and resist the temptation to judge yourself for not practicing self-care in certain areas. The purpose of this check-in with yourself is not to produce guilt, it is to assess how you are doing and to come up with a plan to help care for yourself in meaningful ways.

Put a check mark next to the needs that are basically being met, and a star next to the needs you would like to put some time and effort into meeting:

Physical: need for __ food __ shelter __ clothing __ protection from harm __ exercise __ hygiene.

Medical: need for adequate __ medical __ dental __ mental health care (including regular checkups, preventative care, and treatment of illnesses).

Emotional: need for __ love __ comfort __ empathy __ being valued and encouraged.

Intellectual: need to continue learning through __ education __ a new hobby __ other area of interest.

Spiritual: need to be __ connected to God __ used by him.

Social: need to connect ___ emotionally and ___ intellectually to others in fulfilling ways, and to ___ feel safe in those relationships.

Belonging: need to be part of a group larger than ourselves. This could be fulfilled ___ at work ___ in church ___ with family ___ in close relationships ___ in a larger, meaningful organization.

Giving: need to give to others in ways that contribute to their lives and meet needs in a significant way, such as giving ___ love ___ empathy ___ encouragement ___ care ___ time ___ skills ___ money ___ practical help ___ instruction ___ services.

Significance: need to contribute to the world and make a difference, whether to one person or many. This is often expressed in ___ volunteer work and ___ financial giving.

Your Self-Care Assessment

As you looked at this list of needs, what did you notice? Probably some of your needs are being adequately met and some are not. Don't get overwhelmed; every single thing doesn't have to be fixed now—in fact, they can't be. These areas need to be fine-tuned and paid attention to for the rest of your life. I'm never quite in balance on this myself. I go from less balanced to a little more balanced. Then right when I feel like I'm more in balance, something unforeseen happens in my life and I need to fine-tune some things all over again. If this keeps happening to you, know it is normal, and you're normal.

What might help is noticing what needs are basically being met and which ones could use some attention this week. As you notice your needs, pick one or two unmet needs that jump out at you. Once you identify them it's time to share them with yourself, God, and perhaps others.

Sharing These Needs with Yourself

Step 1: acknowledge an unmet need and take small steps to meet that need. Before we can share our needs with others, we need to acknowledge them as good and valid to ourselves. It's also good to check inside and see if you are waiting for others to meet your needs rather than advocating for yourself. Here are a few good questions to ask yourself:

Am I waiting for others to read my mind about what I need?

Are there times when I don't know what I need, yet I am hoping that someone else will know?

Do I stay silent about a need I have and then feel resentful later because my needs weren't met?

When am I most vulnerable to leaving myself and my needs out of the equation?

In what ways do I already practice self-care in my life?

What things replenish me that I would like to add to my care of myself?

Sharing These Needs with God

Step 2: if you talk to God about things in your life, the next step would be to share your needs with him and ask him to give you wisdom about where to start. Ask him to help you meet your needs as well as see creative solutions you hadn't thought of.

Sharing These Needs with Others

Step 3: if another person is involved in having one or more of your needs met, you may choose to share that need with them. There are some principles that can increase the chances of success. For starters, when sharing your need, say what you want, not just what you're upset about. Be careful here: if you share a need with someone else and just complain about the other person, or how your needs aren't being met, this will never work. I think a part of us wants to believe that we can say anything we want and the other person should be understanding and receptive. But that doesn't work at all . . . at least not with people. The only one who is that patient is God himself. Instead, try these guidelines when sharing your need with someone in your life:

- Calm down (self-soothe) first.
- Keep it simple.
- Do not complain about the other person.
- Say what you want clearly and concisely.
- Be specific.

Here are some examples of healthy ways to share your needs:

I was checking in with myself and realized that I need three hours to myself once a week to recharge. If I don't get this, I can get cranky and resentful . . . and I don't want to be that way. My plan is to do this on Friday mornings and get a babysitter for this time.

I would like to be a little more active, so I'm planning to take a walk after dinner each night. Could you look after the kids for thirty minutes while I do this? I'd be happy to do the same for you when I get back so you can have some time to yourself.

I've always wanted to take a course at the community college. I'm planning to sign up for photography in the fall semester. Do you have any concerns about my doing this that I can address?

I realize I don't spend time reading the Bible like I want to. I've decided to join a Bible study on Thursday mornings because I know I won't do it on my own.

I miss going fishing with the guys. I would like to plan a trip with my friends this summer. Would you be willing to brainstorm with me the timing and best way to do this that works for you too? If you'd like, we could also figure out a time for you to get away with your friends this summer too.

It is important to communicate these desires with an attitude that honors both you and the other person. It is possible that the person you shared your desire with might not say "Great, how wonderful," but that's okay. The need is still important to you. Get more creative with how to meet it and how to enlist friends who might partner with you to accomplish your goal. Remember, it isn't selfish to pursue goals or needs that are important to you. It's actually selfish not to. If you aren't a partner in taking care of your needs, you'll unconsciously be resentful toward others for not meeting your needs . . . often ones you haven't told them about.

Your Self-Care Plan

Even after learning all the ways you can turn toward yourself with self-care, it is normal to remain on autopilot and continue to care for yourself at the minimal level you learned growing up. Changing how you care for yourself takes awareness, intentional thought, and a plan. Consider coming alongside yourself as a compassionate friend. You are totally worth being cared for.

Here are some hints for crafting your plan:

- Begin your self-care plan out of care and compassion for yourself. Look at this as a way to connect to yourself and to provide care in areas of need.
- Choose one of the six areas to focus on: physical, emotional, educational, social, spiritual, or medical.

- Brainstorm all the ways you might care for yourself (for example, physically). Don't censor your list . . . be creative (take a five-minute walk every day, brush and floss your teeth every night, or eat more vegetables).
- Pick the easiest one and be specific. "I'd like to do _____, and have this happen by _____." (For example, take a five-minute walk every day before work).
- Is there anything you need to do or take care of before you can take action on this?
- Decide to try this one goal every day for one week.
- See how it goes and celebrate your progress, even if you did it only one day. Small steps add up!
- See if there is anything you need to change or adjust in order to have more success (maybe get to work ten minutes early every day and take your five-minute walk before you enter the building).
- Try it again for the next week.
- Add something new every week or month, depending on how it is going.
- Congratulate yourself for listening to your needs on the inside and responding to yourself.
- Continue to be aware of simple things you could do to meet your needs in simple ways. Remember: success isn't black and white. Small steps of self-care will make a difference.

Here's an example from my own life. A while back I decided I needed to get into a regular routine of exercise. I hated exercise. I never felt the benefits of the endorphins and was rarely ever glad I did it. I had no discipline or inclination to do this. I only decided to pursue this habit out of care for my body and a desire to stay as healthy as possible. I knew that I could not wait to "want" to go to the gym, so I made a deal with myself. Here's what my progressive list looked like:

Goal: go to the gym three times a week for a class. Progressive plan:

1. Get dressed in gym clothes.
2. Drive to the gym.
3. Go in if I could.
4. Take the class.

Basically, if I did steps 1 and 2, that was a success. If I went in and did the class it was extra. For the first month, about half the time I drove to the gym and drove home again without going in. I celebrated even getting to the parking lot, and considered that a success! Over the next few months, I went in most of the time, though I never enjoyed it or felt glad that I had exercised. However, I was glad to be taking care of myself physically and had been able to find a way to do so that was kind to myself.

My hope for you is to find areas in which you can gradually practice self-care. The motivation is compassion for and connectedness to yourself. You are precious and worth it, and it is not too late to practice self-care in the areas you haven't known how to in the past.

Concluding Reflections

As we come to the close of this chapter, take a moment to check in with yourself about how you are doing. If you would like, ponder the questions below to help process what you've read:

1. What is your response to hearing all the valid reasons it is difficult to practice self-care? Which ones did you relate to?
2. When do you think you stopped caring for yourself?

3. If you took the assessment above, which area would you like to start with to practice self-care? What small step would you like to start with to care for yourself?

4. Try to ask yourself each day: How can I include myself in my day tomorrow? What can I do to honor myself, my needs, and my well-being?

5. Try a compassion moment: "Remember Being Cared For." Remember a time in your life where you were cared for in a meaningful way. It could be a time that you or another person said or did something caring for you that met a deep need inside. If you can't recall one, you can also think of a time you wish someone had noticed your need and responded to you in just the right way. As you remember or imagine this happening, allow yourself to picture this situation: where you are, what you are wearing, how you are standing or sitting, and so forth. Notice the need that was being met and how it felt to have yourself or the other person know you and your need, and then meet that need. Notice how it felt in your body and your soul. Breathe deeply as you experience taking in the good thoughts, feelings, images, and body sensations. If desired, add in positive statements that bring you comfort, such as:

> "It feels good to be seen and responded to in the way I need."
>
> "My needs are normal and are worthy of being met."
>
> "I can become this responsive person to myself."
>
> "I am learning to respond to myself in caring ways."

If you'd like, write your experience in your journal. Include what you remembered, what you or that person said or communicated to you, and how it felt to take that in.

7

Be Compassionate with Your Emotions

Jane couldn't believe she had done it again. This was the third time she had an outburst in a committee meeting and embarrassed herself. She got so frustrated with these people, and after a while she couldn't hold it in anymore! The problem was she ended up looking like the unreasonable one, and her concerns were not addressed. If only she could stop her emotions from getting the best of her.

Making Friends with Your Emotions

Believe it or not, God gave us emotions to help guide us, much like a GPS. When we can see our emotions as giving us valuable information that we can learn and grow from, it helps us be a compassionate friend to ourselves. When emotions come up, it is healthy to stop and listen instead of judging or pushing those emotions away. Instead, step back and ask yourself questions such as:

What is going on inside me?

What do I need?

What message is this emotion sending that I need to address?

What can I do to address the problem my emotions are letting me know exists?

How can I help soothe and calm myself in this moment?

For many of us, the above responses to our emotions are not our instinctual reactions. Instead, we may gloss over our emotions, react strongly to them, push them down, or go numb. These responses occur because we haven't learned healthy ways to process our emotions; consequently, we repeat what we've learned growing up even if it's not effective.

What Does Emotional Maturity Look Like?

Emotional maturity means allowing ourselves to notice and have emotions (even the upsetting ones), name them if possible, and express them in ways that are not harmful to ourselves or others. This process helps lower the intensity of these emotions and calms our system down. When we do this, we will be more connected to ourselves and often will move through these emotions more quickly. Understanding our emotions reduces confusion, increases connection to ourselves, and helps us come up with solutions—all parts of being emotionally mature. Having emotional maturity helps us realize that feelings are not bad; instead, it is the actions we take when we are having strong emotions that can get us into trouble, not the emotions themselves.

Emotions can be complicated and layered. It is normal for a situation, even a positive one, to bring up a variety of emotions all at one time. When multiple emotions come up at the same time, it is common to feel confused. For example, I can be simultaneously excited about getting married, nervous about this new direction of my life, sad about giving up some of the freedoms I've enjoyed, and greatly anticipating going through life with my new spouse. It is healthy to let ourselves have all these emotions and accept them as normal responses to big changes in our life. God has no problem with the emotions we feel. He created emotions to guide us, enrich us, connect us, and to help us experience life more fully—in both the good and bad times.

Working compassionately with our emotions will help us make better choices about how we express those emotions to others in words and actions. Approaching our emotions with a curiosity about what they have to say and teach us is pivotal in both treating ourselves with compassion and coming to our own aid when distressed. One of the ways to understand how we currently interact with our emotions is to take a look at how we were taught to deal with them in the first place.

Four Ways to Respond to Emotions

We have all gone to "emotion school" whether we realize it or not. Knowing how to handle our emotions is not innate, it is learned. From the moment we are born, we are taught by those around us what to do with our emotions. Our parents and others with influence over us passed on what they were taught themselves.

In his book *Raising an Emotionally Intelligent Child*, Dr. John Gottman shares about the four parenting styles that affect children's understanding of what they are feeling and their ability to express those emotions in healthy or unhealthy ways.[1] In order for children to see themselves and their emotions in a positive light, they must see their emotions as good and be given tools to express them in healthy ways. This healthy approach is what Dr. Gottman calls "emotion coaching."[2] This parenting style helps children understand and accept what they are feeling while also learning how to control their behavior.

This is of vital importance because most of us currently respond to our own emotions in the same way we were taught to handle them growing up. As you learn what type of emotion parenting style you were raised with, it will help you learn how to be a compassionate emotion coach to yourself now.

Following are the four basic ways parents tend to respond to a child's emotions and behaviors. Notice how your emotions were responded to growing up. Also be aware that these are four ways you can respond to your own emotions and behavior now.

Emotion Coaching Style

This parent responds to children's emotions by being curious about them. Emotions are not something scary to be dismissed or shut down; they're meant to provide valuable information about the inner life of the child. Parents see children's emotions as a way to connect with them, empathize with them, and help them to come up with solutions to the problem or pain they are facing. By entering the world of the child, the parent will help the child feel valuable, seen, and important, and will also help them learn how to modulate emotions and express them in healthy ways. Children will not feel alone with their emotions, and they will learn to comfort themselves as their parents comfort them.

Reading this description may bring a mixture of feelings. It may sound like a dream to have your emotions responded to in this way. It also may bring sadness, hurt, and anger as you reflect on how different your training about your emotions was. Be kind to yourself as you read this section. The purpose is not to torture yourself with what you may have missed out on. Rather, it is to get a glimpse of what healthy emotion coaching looks like so you can respond to your own emotions and behavior in healthy ways now.

Kathy sat at her parenting book club with five of her friends. They were reading a book on how to help children with their emotions. Right after they read a description of the type of healthy responses an emotion coaching parent would have, she felt uneasy. On the one hand it sounded wonderful. Wouldn't it be a blessing to be raised like this? On the other hand she felt pain as she recalled that her experience was almost the exact opposite. As a child, her emotions were ignored until she couldn't hold them in anymore, and then she was punished when she exploded. As she sat in a circle with her friends, Kathy wanted to run out of the room and cry or yell, or something! She wanted to share what was happening on the inside with the other ladies but was sure they wouldn't understand. She didn't say much and just sweated it out until the group was over, then she quickly rushed out, hoping no one would notice.

If Kathy had been able to compassionately coach herself in the moment, she might have said something like this to herself:

Wow, that was rough to read. I feel so upset. I'm not even sure exactly what I'm feeling. I know it doesn't feel good . . . something about that description really hurts. There must be a good reason. It is so hard to hear that I should have received closeness and empathy when I was upset. I know I got the opposite. I felt so alone and had to figure everything out by myself. My life would have been so much easier if my parents had known how to respond to my emotions in the healthy ways the author was talking about. I've had trouble handling my emotions my whole life, and I even have trouble connecting with my own children in this way. I need to be kind to myself now and realize that it isn't too late. The leader of our group said we were going to learn how to respond to our children's emotions in healthy ways, and I can learn to respond to myself in these new healthy ways too. It's okay that I left the group quickly. I did the best I could when I felt overwhelmed and didn't know what else to do.

If Kathy responded to herself in this different way, she would begin the important road of turning toward herself with compassion while taking the steps she needs to learn new ways of interacting with herself with truth and grace.

Dismissing Style

This parenting style responds to emotions by basically ignoring or dismissing them. When children's emotions are dismissed, they learn that they should push those emotions down and feel happy instead. In the process they feel ashamed for having normal emotions and don't learn healthy ways of handling them. This style often carries into adulthood as we repeat those same messages to ourselves when experiencing difficult emotions. We may say things to ourselves such as: *There's no reason to feel sad. You should be able to handle this. Look on the bright side.* All those comments repeated to ourselves say the same thing: *My emotions are no big deal . . . just be happy.* Of course this doesn't work. The emotions we feel are valid and need to be processed in order to connect to ourselves and help ourselves through what is happening. Consider a more compassionate way to respond to yourself, as Andrew did.

Andrew, a children's pastor, sat in the staff meeting in utter disbelief. He had worked for the last three weeks on the senior pastor's assignment to redo the children's summer program. He had followed every aspect the senior pastor requested and was excited to present it to the whole staff. But four minutes into Andrew's presentation, the senior pastor said he'd changed his mind and the church was going to go in a different direction. Not only did Andrew watch his last three weeks' work go up in smoke, he felt like somehow he had made a mistake. His mind was spinning . . . no warning, no conversation. In addition, being told this in front of a whole group of people was especially humiliating. He wanted to run out of the room and crawl in a hole!

At first, Andrew started to talk with himself the old way. *I'm really upset right now about what happened at work. I know I shouldn't be, after all that's how my boss is with everyone. I'm having a bad attitude, and I need to snap out of it.* But then he made a choice to respond in a new way:

> Wait a minute, that doesn't feel very kind. I don't want to dismiss my emotions like I have so many times before. I think I will give myself a break right now. So what's the truth? The truth is that having your boss scrap three weeks of work on a whim, just because he just changed his mind, is really hard. It is frustrating to have someone do that to you without a thought of how that might impact you. I think I feel angry, sad, taken advantage of, and used all at the same time. No wonder I feel upset and down . . . this would be hard for anyone. I've seen it happen to other people on my staff, and it was really hard on them too. I think I'll be kind to myself about what happened and not dismiss my emotions like I have before. I think I'll tell myself, "I'm so sorry this happened to you. You didn't deserve that. You are going to feel lousy for a while, and that's normal." Maybe I can do something to help myself feel better, such as calling my wife or a friend, or leaving after the meeting to go work out. I think I'll take it easy tonight and let my system calm down. I'm not going to pressure myself to figure out what I'm going to do about this right now. I am a valuable person, and I have a lot to offer . . . even if I wasn't treated that way.

Notice how Andrew is moving toward himself with compassion after initially starting to dismiss his feelings. By softening his response, acknowledging the truth, and validating his own experience and emotions, he was able to be an ally to himself and soothe himself. In the past, Andrew would dismiss his feelings and the emotions would build up. This would result in either yelling at his kids, withdrawing from his wife, or downing a six-pack. Andrew took a courageous path that will help him figure out how to handle this situation from an emotionally settled place.

Disapproving Style

This parenting style responds to strong emotions such as anger, fear, or sadness in a very negative way. Emotions themselves are seen as bad and wrong, and the child needs to be disciplined even if there has been no actual misbehavior. Having emotions is seen as misbehavior. Parents who give these messages most likely were given those same messages when they were children. They are repeating what they know, but those responses build distrust within a child, a sense that something is wrong with who they are. This results in difficulties getting along with others, because low self-esteem and inability to modulate emotions get in the way.

These messages carry into adulthood as we say very judgmental things to ourselves about our own emotional responses. We may say things to ourselves such as, *Stop feeling that way. You are bad for feeling this way. You should be able to handle this and not get upset. You're overreacting . . . you're being a baby . . . just shut up!*

All those comments repeated to ourselves say the same thing: *My emotions are bad and wrong, and I'm bad and wrong for having them.* While it may seem that taking a "tough love" approach with ourselves should spur us on to do the right thing, it doesn't actually work. What we experience instead is discouragement, self-contempt, and difficulty in finding solutions to problems. Notice how Karen learned to relate to herself with compassion despite being raised with this disapproving style.

When Karen was little, her mom had a hard time handling it when Karen was angry, afraid, or sad. Whenever she started to have these feelings, her mom would either tell her to stop being angry or she would tell her that there was nothing to be afraid or sad about. She learned over time to try to turn these emotions off, but later they would come out strongly at school or with a friend. Invariably, she'd get into trouble even though she tried so hard to "be good."

Over time Karen learned not to trust herself or her emotions because she was always told she was wrong for having them. She put her trust in others and was frequently hurt and taken advantage of. All those repetitions of turning off her instincts caused her to lose the ability to pay attention to the instincts God had put in her to guide her. As an adult, Karen would talk to herself much like her mom did. When she was sad, angry, or afraid, she would tell herself she was wrong, selfish, and bad for having these feelings. This didn't help much because she was still left with a tornado of feelings inside and no way to process them or calm herself down.

Recently Karen heard a talk at her church about being compassionate to herself concerning what she was feeling and going through in life. Karen realized she was hearing a different way of handling her emotions: by listening to and validating them. It felt a little scary and even wrong to consider, yet another part of her felt hope. When Karen thought about how her emotions had been handled growing up, she felt some compassion for herself. Over time, Karen learned to say things to herself such as:

> I feel sad that my mom wasn't able to just comfort me when I was sad. All I needed was a hug and to be told she was sad for what I was going through. Those feelings I had all my life were healthy, and I did not deserve to be punished for having them. I'm angry that I didn't learn how to manage my emotions growing up. Not knowing how has caused me so much pain in my relationships. When I have strong feelings now, I will stop and listen to myself and say things like, "What is going on here? What happened that felt bad? What do you need?"

As Karen started to interact with herself in compassionate and understanding ways, she learned how to connect with and respond to herself and others in healthy ways. This change didn't happen overnight, but with each compassionate response, it got easier.

Permissive Style

This parenting style responds to a child's strong emotions by allowing them to be expressed without boundaries. This parent is correct in letting the child know that emotions are valuable and should be listened to. Where the imbalance occurs is that the child is not helped to process the emotions, learn from natural consequences, or come up with appropriate solutions to problems. Without guidance from parents or other caretakers, this child gets the message that any behavior is acceptable, and that you are on your own to figure out how to calm down and come up with a solution to the problem at hand. Children who receive this type of emotional training often find it hard to calm down when angry, sad, or upset; find it difficult to keep friends because of all their outbursts; and find it tough to settle down on the inside and learn new things. These children are taught that feelings are good and allowable, but they do not learn how to modulate and calm down emotionally. They also don't learn that inappropriate behaviors have consequences.

Parents who give these messages have most likely been taught those very responses when they were children, or they were so over-controlled as children themselves that anything goes for their children now. This way of responding to a child's emotions causes emotional immaturity, a lack of self-control, and the inability to regulate their own emotions. In addition, these children often experience difficulty with friendships and carry with them a general sense of unhappiness.

These messages carry into adulthood as we say judgmental things to ourselves about our own emotional responses as well as others' responses to us. We may say things to ourselves such as: *My feelings are fine, and other people should be able to handle them. Life is just not fair. People expect too much of me. I shouldn't have to follow the rules that other people have to follow.* They are also left wondering, *Why do I keep losing friends? Maybe there really is something wrong with me.*

The reality is that our emotions are given to us to understand and learn from. At the same time, we are also responsible for how we share those emotions in words and actions, and should do so in ways that don't harm ourselves or another person. If we give in to expressing our emotions without understanding and learning from them (or without considering others who are also being affected), we are continuing a pattern that will hurt our personal and work relationships for years to come. Let's take a look at the journey both Billy and his parents took to respond to their emotions and behavior in healthy ways with compassion, grace, and truth.

Billy just made the call to his parents that they needed to come and pick him up from college because he'd flunked out of his first semester. His parents were really upset, and Billy felt bad that everyone was mad at him. They should understand that the school was treating him unfairly. It wasn't his fault that he didn't get those papers in on time. The instructions weren't clear, and the professors should have reminded him. Maybe when Dad got there he'd convince the dean of students to give Billy another chance.

Billy and his parents don't yet understand that the problem most likely has nothing to do with the college or the professor, or that someone was unfair to Billy. In this case the problem started long ago when Billy's emotional expression was encouraged without accompanying lessons on how to handle his behavior in appropriate and respectful ways. The problems continued when year after year Billy's parents bailed him out of difficulties with his teachers and coaches, always giving him another chance yet not expecting him to follow the rules or live out logical consequences. Billy has been raised to think he is too special, that rules don't apply to him like they do to others, and that others will always bail him out. Without knowing it, Billy has been raised in a very unreal world. As he went out into the real world of college, without his parents, he was shocked by what these "unreasonable" people were expecting of him; he felt wounded and treated unfairly.

After Billy and his parents packed up his dorm room and headed home, they made a wise move. They sought out a family therapist who helped all three of them realize where things went wrong and how to grow through what happened. As Billy and his parents came to realize where things went off course, Billy began to talk to himself with compassion and truth in the following ways:

> It was really hard to get kicked out of college. All my friends know. It feels like the school was so unfair to me. I was just doing what I've always done, turning things in late and begging for extensions. It always worked out before. I'm just starting to realize that teachers and bosses aren't going to let me float along like I always have. It is hard to get used to reality all at once. I wish my parents had helped me get used to it a little at a time. I know they thought they were helping me by always stepping in to rescue me from my messes, but I'm just starting to realize it actually hurt me. I can see now that I tend to give in to my emotions and impulses without thinking. I'm going to work with my counselor to learn how to listen to my emotions and impulses. I want to slow down and think about my actions and what consequences will occur from the choices I make. I'm young, and I can learn a better way. I can turn this around . . . it's not too late.

As Billy's parents begin to realize what has been missing in their parenting and the effect it has had on Billy, they can talk to themselves with compassion and truth in the following ways:

> It's so hard to see Billy flunk out of his first semester of college. We were sure he would straighten up when he went away to school and would follow all the things we've told him to do. We wanted to give him an easier life than we had growing up. We are starting to realize that all the ways we "helped" him actually hurt him. All those times we gave him gas money when he ran

out of his allowance, asked his teachers to give him an exten-
sion with late assignments, and lectured him instead of giving
him consequences ended up causing him to stay an immature
child. It's easy to look back and see where we made mistakes.
We can honestly say that we had only the best of intentions for
Billy, and we love him dearly. It's not too late. We can get help
to learn how to parent him with both love and limits. We can
also work on ourselves and process the pain we carry inside
about the tough times we went through growing up that caused
us to be too easy on Billy. While this has been very hard for us
too, we can see that it is a growth time for all of us.

Notice how Billy and his parents are learning to show both
truth and grace toward themselves. As they apply compassion
for themselves with truth they will all mature emotionally. They
are choosing to get help and grow in the areas they were lacking,
and this will benefit each of them individually and as a family.

Being a Compassionate Emotion Coach to Ourselves

The above examples give us a glimpse of how to talk to ourselves
with both truth and grace regardless of what training we had
growing up. Following are healthy steps we can take to view and
interact with our emotions. This compassionate way of connecting to our emotions is in contrast to dismissing them, disapproving of them, or expressing them in an out-of-balance way.

1. *Be aware of your emotions.* Consider approaching them
   with interest, curiosity, and kindness. Realize it will feel
   odd or even wrong if this is something you aren't used
   to. When you are feeling an emotion, notice it, and say
   something to yourself such as:
   • *I'm feeling something right now, even if I'm not sure
   what it is.*

- *There must be a good reason I'm feeling this way . . . and maybe more than one reason. I'm going to be kind to myself and let that feeling be there.*
- *I'm going to try not to dismiss my feelings, put them down, numb them, or act them out in my behavior.*
- *I'm going to breathe, take a walk, and let myself know I'll be okay.*

These compassionate responses cause us to move toward ourselves with kindness and curiosity. Even a small movement toward ourselves is a wonderful thing and is enough.

2. *Ask gentle questions* to try to understand what is going on, and try to put words with the feelings. Say something to yourself such as:
   - *I want to learn more about what I'm feeling and why.*
   - *Emotions, what are you trying to tell me?*
   - *What are all of the different things I'm feeling?*
   - *What happened right before I started to feel bad?*
   - *Does this remind me of other times I've felt this way?*

   These kinds of compassionate responses show interest in yourself and what you are experiencing. They also build inner trust and relationship as you come alongside yourself as a caring friend would. As you learn to name what you are feeling, you will be able to work through your emotions rather than get stuck in them.

3. *Continue to be an advocate for yourself.* Don't turn on yourself. As you choose to come alongside yourself, gently say things to yourself such as:
   - *I want to help myself get through this; it is really hard and confusing.*
   - *This is a chance to connect with myself and what I am feeling.*
   - *It's okay if I'm just learning and don't know how yet.*

- *It feels good to want to help and be a friend to myself.*
- *I want to be patient with myself rather than judge myself or shut my emotions down. I'm worth the time it takes to figure this out.*

  This is very important because it helps you to not take an adversarial stance toward yourself and your emotions. Your emotions are not to be judged but understood. You are not bad for having them or bad for struggling with them. You are a normal human being who is growing and learning.

4. *Ask yourself: What do I need?* This may be a new question for you. Just asking yourself what you need is a step toward building a caring relationship with yourself. This question acknowledges you exist, you are being affected by something that is going on, and you have needs in this situation that are worthy of being met. As you check in with what you need, ask yourself:

   - *What do I need right now?*
   - *Do I need help with physical needs such as sleep, rest, food, water, or exercise?*
   - *Do I need support and connection spiritually from God right now?*
   - *Do I need emotional support? Do I feel alone in this?*
   - *What is one way to get the support I need right now?*
   - *What are compassionate words I'd like to hear from myself?*

   This is very important because it turns you toward yourself as a good friend. This process helps build a connection with yourself when you are distressed, and it acknowledges that your needs are valid and worthy of being met.

5. *What are some tools I can use* to soothe myself, calm myself, and bring comfort? This is such a vital step. There

are so many difficult things in life that happen that cannot be changed. What does help is taking the time to soothe, calm, and comfort ourselves in ways that help, not harm. Give this a try, and ask yourself:

- *What are some things I've done in the past that bring me comfort?*
- *What type of soothing words do I need to hear from myself right now?*
- *Are there Scriptures or music that would be comforting to me?*
- *Would it help to journal, pray, cry, or take a run?*
- *Would it help to call a friend? If so, who is someone who would listen and be caring to me rather than giving me advice or responding to me in a matter-of-fact way?*

Like a caring friend, you connect with yourself, express empathy, and use tools that help you calm down while you figure out what to do about the situation. (Chapters 8 and 9 include many practical tools and exercises to help soothe ourselves.)

6. *Is there anything about this situation I need to act on now?* Sometimes being able to name and understand your emotions is enough to lower confusion and calm your system down, and no action needs to be taken. Sometimes after processing your emotions, you may discover there is some action or problem solving that needs to happen. Here are some questions you can ask yourself to see if action is needed, and if so, what and when:

- *Do I need to take action* now?
- *Do I need more time to think about or process what happened?*
- *What are several ways I could handle this situation? What might be the result in each situation?*

- *Would it help to get wise counsel to help me figure out what to do? If so, who might I ask?*
- *Is there something I need to do to protect myself, care for myself, or recover from this situation?*

Going through this process helps you come up with solutions that will help you handle or recover from a difficult situation. Many of us were not shown how to wisely and patiently think through possible solutions when facing a problem. We may have been left on our own to figure it out or have witnessed impulsive actions taken without forethought of consequences. Perhaps problems and possible solutions were simply ignored. By taking the time to (1) assess whether any action needs to be taken, and (2) identify some healthy ways to do so, we are actually building a supportive relationship with ourselves.

I hope these steps help you to learn how to become a compassionate emotion coach to yourself regardless of what training you had growing up. This way of responding to your emotions with curiosity, acceptance, and compassion may be new to you. Each small step will make a big difference in your life and relationships.

Concluding Reflections

As we come to the close of this chapter, take a moment to check in with yourself about how you are doing. If you would like, ponder the questions below to help process what you've read:

1. What is one way you can make a small shift in seeing your humanity with acceptance and compassion? What can you say to yourself?
2. What was your response to viewing your feelings as a helpful GPS to guide you?

3. What type of training did you receive about emotions as a child?

___ Emotion Coaching ___ Dismissing ___ Disapproving ___ Permissive

How has this training affected you and your relationships?

4. As you look at the six steps to becoming a compassionate emotion coach to yourself, where would you like to start? What kind of a difference will this make in your life?

5. Try a compassion moment: take a moment for yourself away from distractions. Sit in a comfortable place and talk to yourself with compassion about what you've learned in this chapter:

I had no idea that emotions are so valuable. I've spent most of my life either trying not to feel them or beating myself up for feeling them. This idea that they are placed inside of me by God to help guide me is so new. I'm going to try to be open to this perspective. I'd like to learn how to notice them, learn from them, and respond to them in healthy ways. Even my openness to see emotions as a helpful guidance system is a step in the right direction.

Allow these words to sink in, even a little bit, and notice what it feels like in your body to respond to yourself with kindness and compassion.

8

Practical Tools to Build a Compassionate Relationship with Yourself

arcy closed the link to the article she had been reading about the importance of developing a compassionate relationship with herself. Marcy's Aunt Kate had sent it to her, and Marcy read it because she knew her aunt really did care about her. By the end of the article, Marcy was tentatively agreeing that she both wanted and needed to learn how to give herself a break by approaching herself with compassion. But where should she start? It seemed like an overwhelming task to even begin. You may feel like Marcy too.

In this chapter you will learn several tools you can use to give yourself a break as you build a compassionate relationship with yourself. The tools involve how you view yourself, talk to yourself, and interact with yourself in compassionate ways.

Read over these ideas, and check with yourself on the inside. With some of the ideas presented you may think, *There's no way I can do that right now.* Other ideas will seem like possibilities, and perhaps one or two will have you thinking, *Okay, I could do that one.* Start there. Everyone will respond differently to this material. Trust your gut and begin where you can.

However, I don't want you to focus on one idea that isn't right for you right now and then give up. That's not being a good friend to yourself. Start where you are, and begin to build these skills.

How We View Ourselves Is Paramount

We are all in the same boat. We all struggle. We all have frailties, weaknesses, and imperfections. How we view these human qualities will determine the kind of relationship we have with ourselves, with God, and with others.

In order to be compassionate with ourselves, we need to be reconciled with ourselves. This means that we come to accept the reality that we are not perfect and are not supposed to be. We often live as if we should be perfect, and we are devastated when we fail, don't know everything, misjudge a situation, are selfish, "lose it," and so on.

It's time to let that one go! Being imperfect is part of being human. This doesn't mean that we stop learning and growing. What it means is that we accept our humanity; take those sins, mistakes, and shortcomings to God for forgiveness and healing; and then let those things go, with compassion for ourselves.

Our internal peace does not come from seeing ourselves as strong, without faults, or above making mistakes. Peace of mind comes from accepting our flaws and mistakes. God does not have a bad attitude toward you. He is not surprised by your mistakes and sins. In fact, he loves you and wants you to come to him because he wants to be a part of your life every step of the way . . . the good, the bad, *and* the ugly. He has compassion toward you, and his heart breaks as you suffer and struggle through the difficult parts of life.

> He will not shout or cry out,
>> or raise his voice in the streets.
> A bruised reed he will not break,
>> and a smoldering wick he will not snuff out.
>   (Isa. 42:2–3)

The good news is that we can find compassion and tenderness from God in these vulnerable states. He will not break us or snuff us out because we are struggling. God has unending patience, gentleness, and compassion toward us. He shows his love for us, and this should be our model for interacting with ourselves. Try to breathe this truth in a little bit, and say to yourself:

> How could this be? I thought God looked down on me and got mad at me for doing the wrong thing and for struggling over and over. There is a place inside that really wants to believe that he actually has compassion for my struggles and wants to help me. I can't totally believe this deep down, and he understands that too. I think I will just consider that this could be true. I can feel a tiny bit of hope and warmth inside at this possibility. It's okay for me to be "in process" about this.

Shift to a Positive Stance

A slow shift toward treating ourselves like a best friend needs to happen. It's fine if right now you're thinking, *I can't even imagine treating myself like a best friend.* That's okay. If you feel this way, it means you're being honest, and that's where you are right now. Here's a sample of a way your thinking can change over time:

I don't see myself being able to interact with myself as a best friend, and I can't imagine that ever being true.

I can't imagine ever treating myself as a best friend, but I wish I could.

I can't imagine ever treating myself as a best friend, but I'm willing to try.

I'd like to see myself as a best friend, so I'll start by speaking to myself kindly and see how it goes.

Accepting where you are and moving one small step at a time is being a best friend. That's what best friends do: they accept and love you where you are and encourage you to believe that there is hope and that you can make small changes. Here are some other qualities of a compassionate best friend:

- Gives you truth and grace.
- Is understanding.
- Gives you permission to "be."
- Provides accountability with grace.
- Compliments and encourages you on a regular basis.
- Forgives faults.
- Has fun with you.
- Listens to your thoughts, feelings, and needs.

Even if it doesn't feel like it right now, you can learn over time, in small steps, how to become your own compassionate best friend. Imagine how nice it will be to carry an encouraging friend around inside of you. I've gone through this process myself, and it provides me with a sense of stability, calm, and connectedness that affects my life every day in positive ways.

How does this play out? It means we are not surprised when we make mistakes, sin, or don't have everything figured out. It means we accept these failures and mistakes, and even see them as part of the process. It means we don't condemn ourselves for our failures; instead we handle them in a healthy manner.

This means taking these problems to God and asking for forgiveness from him and others when necessary. It means granting ourselves and others kindness, understanding, and help when we fail. It means surrounding ourselves with supportive people, not ones who tear us down. If we don't have those trusted kinds of people close at hand, we'll work to find them and develop relationships. I have seen many, many people find this kind of safe place in support groups led by well-trained therapists or leaders who establish a safe environment in which to grow.

Change the Way You Talk to Yourself

For as he thinketh in his heart, so is he. (Prov. 23:7 KJV)

Often, a lot of our distress comes from the way we interact with ourselves. The way we speak to ourselves about our own human frailties, sins, and imperfections has a direct impact on our peace of mind. Self-compassion means learning to develop a loving and accepting dialogue with ourselves—especially when we've failed. This is in contrast to the other messages we give ourselves, such as: *That was stupid. What's wrong with me? I need to try harder. I'm a loser.*

What are the fruits of these comments? Shame, guilt, and even less ability to do what we were attempting. We say these things with the hope they will motivate us to do better, but they do not. What we need is grace from God and ourselves, not shame and condemnation.

Sometimes it's easy to figure out where these negative messages come from, and sometimes it's not. We may be repeating critical messages that were said to us by others. We may be repeating conclusions we made as children when our needs weren't met or difficult things happened to us. We may be reflecting the reality of living in a world where we are constantly judged and evaluated . . . about everything! If you know why you respond to yourself with these negative messages, you can speak to yourself by saying:

> I now have a better idea of why I say these negative things to myself when I mess up. When I was growing up, my normal mistakes and failures were treated with disdain and criticism. No wonder I'm so hard on myself. I accepted these negative conclusions about myself as true because I didn't have any other example or way of being compassionate toward myself in those moments. I am starting to feel a little compassion for that small child who went through all that criticism. I want to be different with myself when I fail, make a mistake, or just don't know what to do.

In contrast, we may not be able to figure out why we beat ourselves up. No matter what, know that those messages have developed in our minds for a reason. People do not just draw negative conclusions about themselves out of the blue. Sometimes those conclusions were made before we had visual conscious memories (before age four).

Please take a compassionate stance toward yourself about this. Those messages are there for a reason. See if you can feel some compassion for yourself, knowing that these negative messages have been active in your life for a while. Here's a caring way to respond to yourself:

> I still cannot figure out why I am so hard on myself. Those messages must be there for a reason. Even if I am unable to figure it out, I can still take steps to change the way I speak to myself. For now, I will let myself know that I am sorry I have been speaking

to myself in this way; I am committed to walking down a different path when I notice these self-critical messages coming up.

———

To truly be at peace with ourselves, we accept grace, forgiveness, and acceptance from God then extend them to ourselves out of his love for us. You may understandably be wondering, *How do I start to change the way I talk to myself?*

1. *Notice the way you talk to yourself.* We can't change what we aren't aware of. You may be surprised by how much time you spend saying negative things to yourself. Keep a paper in your purse or pocket, and write down all the comments you say to yourself, both positive and negative, for two days.

2. *Check out what you said to yourself.* Don't just accept it as true. Ask yourself:
   - *Is what I'm saying to myself true?*
   - *What would others in this situation say to themselves?*
   - *What other possible conclusions could be made in this situation?*
   - *What would the kindest person I know say to me about this situation?*

3. *Based on the above input, craft a new, kinder response to yourself.* Here are some examples:
   - *I know that I called myself "stupid" for not returning that call to my boss. I don't think that was really stupid. I think I am overwhelmed with work and couldn't add one more thing to my to-do list right then. I can still call her back tomorrow. I'm not a stupid person at all. I'm a smart, capable person who was overwhelmed.*
   - *I know I feel bad about not being more patient with my kids. I really want to raise them differently than I was*

raised. The reality is that even though I'm not perfect or even close to it, I still have more patience and compassion for my kids than I received. I think I'll notice both: wanting to do better and also giving myself credit for the strides I have made.

- *I feel horrible that my kids saw me drunk again last night. I swore I wouldn't do that again. I don't want them to have to worry about me, take care of me, and be alone because I'm intoxicated. There must be a reason I keep doing this. I'm going to get help to figure out and work through the underlying pain that causes me to drink to numb my feelings.*

Protect Yourself from Negative Influences

> Above all else, guard your heart,
>   for everything you do flows from it. (Prov. 4:23)

We've been working on changing any negative influences that come from within ourselves by transforming the ways we talk to ourselves. It's also important to reduce, remove, or stop any negative influences from the outside that tear us down.

My husband, Dave, a Bible scholar, shared with me the following concept of stewardship in this regard. Stewardship is one of the basic elements of New Testament teaching. Christians are responsible to God to be good stewards of the things he has lent us—which is everything (see Rom. 14:4; 1 Cor. 4:1–5; 2 Cor. 5:6–15; Titus 1:7; 1 Pet. 4:10). This stewardship principle explains why we should avoid all damage to self if possible (for example, the Bible says we should run away from persecution if possible and not volunteer for mistreatment, though there are exceptions to this general rule in the Bible).[1]

God wants us to be good stewards of what he has given us. We often apply this to the things and people he has given to us in our life: our possessions, family, ministry, friends, job, and so forth. Unfortunately, we don't tend to apply this principle to being a good steward of ourselves. Being a good steward of ourselves involves caring for our minds, bodies, spirits, and emotional health. This includes nurturing ourselves as well as protecting ourselves in all of these ways, including setting boundaries.

Setting boundaries with those who tear you down is extremely important. Allowing people in your life to criticize you or harm you causes much damage to your soul and self-esteem. There is no way to completely remove these influences from your life; however, there are ways you can reduce these conversations and advocate for yourself. Imagine yourself hanging out with a good friend of yours. While you're talking, someone comes up, starts putting your friend down, and tells him all the awful things that are wrong with him. You hear this, and you notice yourself starting to get angry. You want to come to your friend's defense. It is a normal mechanism to desire to protect and advocate for those being bullied and mistreated.

Now imagine that the person being treated this way is you. Part of building a compassionate relationship with yourself is to be your own best friend and advocate for yourself in the way you would for a friend who was being harmed. What might it look like to set a boundary with someone who is harming you? What could you say?

"Stop. I can tell you are upset with me about something. I'd be happy to talk with you about it but not if you are going to yell, criticize, and put me down. You need to decide right now if you can calm yourself down and speak to me with respect. Otherwise this conversation is over." If the person keeps going, leave the situation. While this may sound simplistic and may not work for every situation, it is doable and empowering.

What I'd like you to notice is that being your own best friend means advocating and/or removing yourself from damaging situations. Covering detailed strategies for doing this is beyond the scope of this book. If you'd like to learn more about this, I recommend *How to Have That Difficult Conversation* by Henry Cloud and John Townsend.

Remember that progress in this area comes a little at a time. Its progression may look like this:

I let the person criticize me and don't stand up for myself. I feel powerless and don't know what to do. I blame myself and put myself down too.

I let the person criticize me and don't stand up for myself. I feel powerless and don't know what to do. I tell myself I didn't deserve that.

I let the person criticize me and don't stand up for myself. I feel powerless and don't know what to do. I tell myself I didn't deserve that, and I come up with a plan for what to do next time.

I let the person criticize me and don't stand up for myself. I feel less powerless and try to stand up for myself, but it doesn't work.

The person starts to criticize me. I put my hand up and say, "Stop," and walk away.

The person starts to criticize me. I put my hand up and say, "Stop. I can tell you are upset with me about something. I'd be happy to talk with you about it but not if you are going to yell, criticize, and put me down. You need to decide right now if you can calm yourself down and speak to me with respect. Otherwise this conversation is over." If this person does not learn from my boundaries, I greatly limit my encounters with them and/or stop this relationship if appropriate.

Remember to remind yourself: *I am worthy of respect, kind treatment, and protection from the negative actions of others as well as from myself.*

Here's a kind way of talking to yourself about caring for yourself as a good steward:

Wow. I never knew that I am called to be a steward of **myself**. In some ways this makes so much sense, yet it seems so new. I want to learn how to do this, and it feels so good to know that God wants this for me as well. The fact that he sees me as valuable and worthy of kindness, compassion, and care makes a big difference.

Practice Interacting with Yourself in Compassionate Ways

Here are some tools you can use to infuse yourself with compassion. Developing and growing this compassionate part of you takes practice. A little bit at a time is just fine.

Take in Positive Experiences

Exercise 1: soak in something positive that is happening in your life right now.[2] Our human brain tends to remember the bad more often than the good. Actively taking in good experiences is an important part of being compassionate with yourself.

1. Think of something positive that is currently happening in your life. It could be something as simple as sunshine, food to eat, a baby's smile, a nice bed to sleep in, a beautiful sunset, good friends, or a recent positive experience.
2. Recognize that there are good things happening in your life.
3. Soak this truth in. Tell yourself there are good things to absorb.
4. Allow yourself to soak that good experience in at an even deeper level. Breathe it in through your whole body.

5. Attach some words to it that are meaningful and bring comfort to you. *Maybe I do have good things in my life. I can take in blessings that are happening to me and I can rest in the good that is in my life.*

6. Notice sensations of relaxation, peace, or contentment in your body as you soak in the good.

7. Take a snapshot in your mind of this truth to come back to at a later time.

If you'd like, write your experience in your journal. Include what you remembered, what the truth and goodness was, and how it felt to soak that in.

Exercise 2: record caring and compassionate experiences in a compassion journal. Look for occasions where good is happening right now, and write these experiences in a compassion journal to reflect on.

Here's how this works: deliberately bring to mind the experience of being cared about and receiving compassion when you are going through challenging situations. Write them down. These can be compassionate statements you say to yourself; ones you hear from others; or ones you hear from time spent with God in his Word, through prayer, or through walking in nature with him. This is a concrete way to record times of encouragement and compassion.

Make four columns. Write down:

1. What is the situation/circumstance?
2. Who gave you this encouragement?
3. What truth was shared?
4. What does it sound like rewritten in your own words?

After you rewrite these truthful, compassionate statements about yourself, close your eyes and breathe those statements in wholeheartedly. Take them in as truth about your worth and value. See if you can breathe them in at a little deeper level each time. You can also include Scriptures that are meaningful to you (see appendix A). Include anything that comes to you—past or present—that touches this inner critic in you that needs affirmation and encouragement.

Here is encouragement from me to you that you can add to your journal:

> You are a delightful person who is learning how to be compassionate with yourself. Good for you. Don't stop. It is my greatest wish that you are able to turn away from being hard on yourself or ignoring yourself and become your own best friend. Your efforts will pay off as you learn to nurture and value yourself more and more each day.

Learn to Let the Pain Go

It is very common to ruminate about pain and harm that has been done to us. Often we can't seem to let go of it. It is important to feel the reality of that pain as part of processing it. Our goal is to learn what we can from the experience and then let it go. But it's no surprise that we often get stuck on the "letting go" part.

It is not kind or compassionate toward ourselves to ruminate over the case we have against another person. Sadly, we are the ones who are harmed by this process, and we often don't realize the cost of not letting things go.

Lots of negative emotions can cause bitterness and hardness of heart.

These take an enormous amount of time and energy to manage.

This drains us and gives us a negative outlook on the world.

Not letting things go contributes to chronic stress, which has devastating effects on our body, soul, and mind, as well as on our relationships.

Whatever we are carrying will leak out onto others we love even if we try hard not to let it.

This can also make us self-absorbed, takes precious energy to keep contained, and stops us from taking in and enjoying the good things that are there.

If you are in this spot, no doubt you have already worked hard at trying to let it go. What does letting it go mean? Am I saying what happened was no big deal? Absolutely not. It means that we're done with continuing to suffer over what happened. The original injury was horrible, but the fallout we get stuck in is devastating as well. Consider learning ways to let things go—not as a way of minimizing what happened, but as a way of ending the destructive cycle of paying for it.

The following ideas might help you let go. If they are not enough, I encourage you to contact a therapist who has been trained in a special kind of therapy called EMDR (Eye Movement Desensitization and Reprocessing; www.emdria.org or www.emdr.com) to help you get unstuck. Sometimes difficult life experiences get stuck in our brains, literally, and EMDR is an effective way to help your brain get unstuck. Another great resource is *Getting Past Your Past: Take Control of Your Life with Self-Help Techniques from EMDR* by Francine Shapiro.

Here is a "letting go" exercise to try now if you'd like. First, let yourself notice the case you have against this person. Notice what you may get out of keeping this pain alive (maybe a sense of validation that something genuinely bad happened, a way to ward off feelings of helplessness, or the only way you know to seek justice for the situation). Notice the costs to you. One way to help with this is to think about what your life, thoughts, emotions, energy, and so forth would be like if you no longer had this unresolved pain with this person or yourself.

Second, allow the pain to wash out of you by imagining standing under a gentle waterfall or shower stream. Allow the water to cleanse you and wash away the pain you carry. Let it flow and naturally cleanse you inside and out. Say to yourself, *I can let a little of this go now. I don't have to carry all of it.* If you find it difficult to let some of it go, say to yourself, *I can let a little bit of it go now. As I practice, I can imagine letting a little more of this go sometime in the future . . . when the time is right.*

This is not a one-time exercise. Practice this often through imagery and/or while actually in the shower. If you'd like, write your experience in your journal. Include what the pain looked like; where some of it went; what it was like in your body, soul, and mind to release some of it; what words you repeated to yourself; and what it is like to have a tiny bit less of it now.

Don't Hold Things against Yourself

It is very common to ruminate about pain and harm that we have caused either intentionally or accidentally. Many people find it very difficult to forgive themselves and move on. It is important to feel the reality of what has happened in order to learn what we can from the experience and let it go.

It is not kind or compassionate toward ourselves to ruminate over the case we have against ourselves. This actually keeps us stuck and harms us.

Exercise 1: try visualizing a blackboard with a list of the things you haven't been able to forgive yourself for. List these with a few words each—no paragraphs! Then imagine a shining figure, the Lord himself, sweeping a sponge or damp cloth across the blackboard, wiping it clean. See his face smiling with love and acceptance. Say to yourself, *The Lord has forgiven me for my sins and mistakes.* Have him wipe the board clean as many times as you need him to. *The Lord has forgiven my sins and mistakes.* Then begin the process of forgiving yourself.

Go up to the blackboard with the Lord and have him take your hand in his as you and he together wipe the board clean.

Repeat this as many times as is necessary. Thank God that 1 John 1:9 is true: "If we confess our sins, he is faithful and just and will forgive us our sins and purify us from all unrighteousness." Thank God for his unending forgiveness, love, and acceptance. Rest in his arms, and soak up his acceptance and delight in you. It is very normal to repeat this exercise many times, with the goal that a little more is erased each time. Remember this is a process, not a one-time experience.

If you'd like, write your experience in your journal. Include what the blackboard looked like; what it felt like to see Jesus wipe it clean; and what it was like in your body, soul, and mind to wipe that board clean and release the guilt or shame of it. Also write what positive words you repeated to yourself. Soak in this experience—even if only one or two wrongs were erased.

Exercise 2: complete the letting go exercise shared in the previous section, except this time apply it to the wrongs you hold against yourself. As you reflect on this chapter, notice all the different ways you can slowly learn to interact with yourself as a compassionate friend. Making small changes in a variety of areas can have a big impact on treating yourself with compassion.

Taking small steps to talk to yourself with kindness can help your inner critic's voice get smaller.

Protecting yourself from harm honors you as the precious person God created, and builds that compassionate relationship with yourself.

Noticing and taking in positive experiences in your life helps build calmness inside and helps you notice the good that is happening in your life.

Learning ways to slowly let go of pain you've been carrying lessens the load you carry, and makes more room inside for compassion, grace, and good things.

Concluding Reflections

As we come to the close of this chapter, take a moment to check in with yourself about how you are doing. If you would like, ponder the questions below to help process what you've read and experienced:

1. What was it like to learn that part of giving yourself a break is accepting the reality that we aren't perfect and, in fact, we aren't supposed to be?

2. What was it like to realize that you can make changes to your view of yourself in small steps?

3. Ask yourself, *What situations or people do I allow in my life that put me down in ways that are damaging to me? What is one small step I can take to be a best friend to myself in these situations?*

4. What exercises were the most helpful for you? How did they help?

5. When can you practice the exercises that made a difference to you on a regular basis?

9

Practice Self-Soothing Techniques

My heart was pounding as I pulled off to the side of the road. I had just witnessed a serious car accident that I would have been involved in had I entered the intersection three seconds earlier. My heart and mind were racing. That could have been my car rolling over three times before landing against that utility pole! Many people had witnessed this accident and rushed to help, so I wasn't needed. But how could I possibly drive to work and counsel people when I was feeling so distressed? After pulling off the road, I put my car in park and took some slow deep breaths while saying calming truths to myself. *I'm okay . . . I'm upset, but I can calm down . . . let me give myself time to soothe my system. God has me in his hands. He will help me work this afternoon or help me cancel my appointments if I need to . . . just breathe.*

As I did this, my body and mind slowly returned to normal, and after about fifteen minutes I was able to drive to work and counsel with my clients. Knowing how to be there for myself in the moment helped to ground me so that I could be compassionate with myself. Then I was able to be there for others.

When distressed, our brain and body go into overdrive trying to cope with whatever is going on. This causes our system to overload physiologically, so we all need ways to transition from distress to calm. The ability to self-soothe as well as to employ emotional regulation techniques are the skills that help with this transition. When practiced, our emotions, thoughts, body responses (heart rate, blood pressure, sweat), and behavior calm down to a manageable level. We are then able to respond in a comforting, nurturing, and gentle way to ourselves, especially in moments of distress or agitation. The ability to self-soothe is a central part of a mature emotional life.

The need for self-soothing strategies occurs at all ages for all people. This journey begins as babies suck on pacifiers and clutch soft blankets as they learn to modulate their anxiety when distressed. We aren't born knowing how to self-soothe. One of the main ways we learn is by experiencing and observing how our parents or caretakers respond to our needs. Self-soothing practices are the ways we calm ourselves as we learn to tolerate and reduce the sensations of distress that accompany an unmet need or distressing experience.

Sally wanted another cookie. She loved chocolate chip cookies and was quite insistent on consuming as many as possible. Her mom knew that one was enough, and she also knew that she was in for a tussle as she set this boundary with Sally. "Honey, I know you want another cookie, and you are so hoping I'll say yes, even though you know you can only have one. Cookies are truly wonderful, and I'm saying no to another one because too many aren't good for you." Sally first pouted, then cried, then turned away. Her mom gave Sally a little more empathy while keeping her boundary. She also did some slow, deep breathing to calm herself and talk to herself with compassion:

> It's so hard to be a balanced mom. I know I'm doing the right thing. Sally needs to learn how to delay gratification. It sure is hard to be the mom setting the boundary. I'm doing a good job because I'm helping her learn to cope with being disappointed. She'll be all right. I'll be all right too.

As in the above example, when we are distressed what helps is having the other person see our need, feel bad with us, and respond to us in kind and comforting ways. Even though the expressed need isn't met (for example, wanting another cookie), the child knows they have been heard and are cared about. The ability to self-soothe develops as the child learns, over time, that they will be all right and can calm down when something difficult or disappointing happens. Ideally, parents impart the ability to self-soothe by:

Validating their child's needs: "Yes, I know you want to go to your friend's house."

Empathizing with their emotions: "You are angry and sad that you can't go to Billy's house before you do your homework."

Providing physical affection (hugs, holding, kisses, being together), especially when the child is distressed.

Making eye contact, whether pleased or upset with their child.

Offering words of encouragement and reassurance: "I know you are discouraged. I want you to know I believe in you, will stand by you, and know you'll get through this."

When children receive these responses, they feel validated that their needs are normal, and they experience being soothed in their discomfort and disappointments. Over time, they learn to

offer *themselves* words of compassion, empathy, and encouragement. Adults need these types of responses just as much—not
only from others, but from themselves. It is encouraging to
know we can learn to validate ourselves in these ways. There
are times, however, when more than self-compassion is needed.

A Special Challenge: Repetitive Distressing Situations and Trauma

The difficulties of life require lots of compassion, comfort, understanding, and kindness. For many of us, these difficulties
have been met with indifference, blame, or ineffective attempts
by others to help. Most people have experienced traumatic and
repeated distressing situations. These can range from one-time
traumatic events to living with chronic stress from a variety of
sources. Examples of the latter include living in an environment with alcohol or substance abuse issues, financial problems,
losses, learning disabilities, or an unhappy marriage, neglect,
arguing, bullying, violent behavior, as well as verbal, sexual, or
physical abuse.

In my counseling practice, I see many people who are stuck
in habits, reactions, and behaviors due to not having fully processed upsetting or distressing events in their lives. When these
build up over time, they can become traumatic for the person. I
define *trauma* as any experience or set of repetitive experiences
that overwhelms a person's system emotionally and physically.
Trauma is not only the extreme events most would label traumatic, such as a plane crash, assault, war, or bank robbery.
Trauma may also occur when a person is subjected to the effects
of prolonged distressing events.

I often think of this analogy. If I were to try to pour a gallon
jug of water into a sixteen-ounce cup, the cup would overflow all
over the place. There is nothing wrong with the cup. It is simply

146

not made to hold a gallon of liquid. That is what happens with trauma. Our systems are made to handle a significant amount of distress. When an experience or series of repetitive distressing experiences occur, those excess experiences are stored in our body, mind, and emotions. That's why we overreact physically and emotionally to certain triggers that are similar in some way to the prior distressing experiences we have gone through. Our cup overflows.

It is important to understand that our *entire being* is affected when exposed to extreme or repetitive stress. Our brains and bodies are activated in a variety of areas to deal with these situations. In addition, our immune system, gastrointestinal system, and the sense of being comfortable in our own body are affected.

Many times our systems do not "reset" themselves and go back to normal. As a result, many people's systems are hyperaroused, living in the old trauma while preparing to respond to the next difficult situation. All of this is automatic and not under conscious control.

When we undergo extreme stress, our brain shuts down, and the entire picture of what happened does not become stored coherently in our brain. Instead, we store what has happened in pieces—images, sights, sounds, smells, emotions, thoughts about ourselves and others, and physical sensations. The event is not remembered as a coherent story of what happened long ago. Instead, if and when a similar event occurs in the here and now, all those old residual thoughts, feelings, and body sensations that are stuck in our system are activated; we then experience these in the present moment as if they are happening right now. This is what happens when we are "triggered" by a current situation, which can easily happen with everyday occurrences.

Jerry was about to explode. Sherrie had asked him to pay the bills for the third time in as many days. *She doesn't trust me*, he thought. *She's always after me . . . why doesn't she just give me some space. I should give her a piece of my mind!* Jerry's strong reaction was much greater than was warranted. Because he'd grown up with a critical father and an anxious mother who had micromanaged him in an attempt to quell their own anxiety, Jerry had a storehouse of pain, disrespect, and frustration built up inside just waiting to be unleashed on anyone who made a request or questioned him in even the slightest way.

In the past, Jerry would have given Sherrie a piece of his mind, escalating a small event into a huge argument that would last for days. This time, however, he decided to respond to Sherrie differently. "You asking me to pay the bills is bugging me. Let me take a moment to calm myself before responding to you." He then excused himself to interact with himself in compassionate ways. He took a slow walk in the neighborhood, and he said to himself:

> I'm really bugged that Sherrie asked me to pay the bills again. It feels like growing up, when I was nitpicked all the time. Let me breathe and think this through. I know Sherrie loves me and doesn't want to bug me. It's true that she has asked me three days in a row and I haven't paid them yet. I probably need to take a look at why I'm putting that off. I'm not going to unleash all my frustration on her. It is hard to be reminded of something I haven't done, yet she doesn't deserve a harsh reaction. I'll pay the bills tonight and respond to her kindly. I'm not a bad guy for my initial reaction. It just reminds me how hard it was growing up to have someone all over me about the littlest things. I feel good that I'm taking the time to calm myself down and respond to Sherrie with respect.

Just like Jerry, most people are doing an amazing job trying to manage a system that has been changed and compromised by the effects of unresolved trauma and pain. Despite their heroic efforts to live a functional and fulfilling life, there are still lingering symptoms that steal joy, spontaneity, and peace from life. If you can relate to this section, you may find yourself experiencing some of the following symptoms:

- Difficulty being fully present in the moment.
- Difficulty experiencing pleasure or relaxation in the present moment.
- A tense body in a state of hyperalertness.
- Agitation and anxiety experienced in body and mind.
- Constant alertness to respond to the next potentially hurtful situation.
- Times of overreacting to a current situation without knowing why (such as responding to an event that is a "three" level of distress as if it were an "eight").
- Persistent feelings of being out of control, not good enough, moody, agitated, anxious, and/or hopeless.
- Trouble paying attention, fitting in, and/or noticing the needs of others.

For the majority of people, who can relate to being affected by trauma or prolonged stress, learning to self-soothe and practice self-care with compassion is of the utmost importance. This makes sense. If our system is still on alert, the idea of relaxing and self-soothing will be very foreign. In fact this will be the opposite of how our system is preparing itself. The good news is we can learn how to do this in lots of ways. That is what the rest of this chapter is all about. (You can also download more ideas of how to interact with yourself in healthy ways when you get triggered by going to www.kimfredrickson.com and downloading the handout "Soothing Yourself When Distressed" under "free articles.")

Learning to soothe our body, mind, spirit, and emotions is key to reclaiming our whole system from the effects of the past.

Not only will we learn to calm our system in a variety of ways, we will also learn that we can take effective action to help ourselves, rather than feel like we are powerless to resist the effects of the past.

Recovery from trauma is about reclaiming ourselves, empowering ourselves, reconnecting to ourselves with compassion, and establishing safe connecting relationships with ourselves, God, and others. If you responded to what was shared in this section, here's something you might say to yourself:

> I had no idea that what I've been through is considered trauma. It is validating to learn that going through something hard, over and over, has had real effects on me. It explains so much why I haven't made more progress in these automatic thoughts, feelings, and reactions I sometimes have. It feels good to know it isn't about me doing this wrong. I'm looking forward to learning soothing ways to retrain myself.

When we haven't learned how to soothe ourselves in healthy ways, we tend to do whatever we've been taught or shown by others when we were young. No one plans to use unhealthy practices to soothe themselves. The more difficulties, disappointments, and disturbing life experiences a person has gone through, the more soothing of unprocessed pain they will need.

Often the anxiety-reducing tools we happened upon as a child or adolescent are the ones we continue to use into adulthood. Unfortunately, many of these cause us harm as we try to soothe pain or emptiness in the moment. These habits tend to fall into two categories:

1. *Substances we ingest* to reduce our anxiety (such as food, alcohol, and legal or illegal drugs).

2. *Mood-altering behaviors* we practice to reduce our anxiety (such as excessive video games, computer use, television, gambling, sexual activity, reading, exercising, or shopping;

eating disorders; smoking; pornography; overwork; isolating through withdrawal; controlling our environment; or busyness with projects).

Marsha found herself in front of the refrigerator again. She was back to nibbling and grazing on ice cream, cookies, or leftover pizza. Without meaning to, she found herself eating to soothe the loneliness she felt. As long as she could remember, she had felt alone and unseen. As a child she had never fit in, and as an adult she felt disconnected in her relationships. *Why am I doing this again? I hate myself afterward. It only helps in the moment, and then I step on the scale. But no matter how hard I try—and I do—I keep repeating this emotional eating.*

It would be easy to substitute drinking, pornography, being on the computer all the time, or even excessive reading in the above story. Anything done *in excess* can turn into a mood-altering behavior. The common link is that we feel we must do this behavior to reduce anxiety and/or fill the emptiness inside. Just like Marsha, our attempts to stop the behavior have failed, even when it is clear that it is harming our physical, emotional, spiritual, and relational health.

Before you get down on yourself, remember that we are all in the same boat. We all happened upon unhealthy behaviors in an attempt to handle the difficulties of life. God understands. He also wants us to care for ourselves and turn to him to find healthy ways to reduce our anxiety, sadness, anger, and loneliness. Part of being compassionate with yourself means you recognize that some of the unhealthy choices you made were not made in a vacuum.

Based on this new understanding, here's something you can say to yourself:

I had no idea that the unhealthy ways I've been using to soothe the pain, emptiness, and aloneness I feel developed because

I didn't know what else to do. These patterns I've developed have been locked in for a very long time. That doesn't mean it is hopeless or that it's too late. It does mean that rather than just trying to stop coping in unhealthy ways, I can start learning new ways to soothe and care for myself in compassionate ways. It's all so new, and it gives me hope.

Specific Self-Soothing Techniques

Following are some techniques for self-soothing in order to help you to connect with yourself on the inside. In addition, these techniques will help you reduce emotional reactions and behaviors that may harm you and your relationships. This is a very important way of developing self-compassion. These techniques are meant to calm, comfort, and soothe. On the rare occasion when they don't, use the Container Exercise near the end of this chapter to temporarily store any distressing feelings until you can talk to a therapist or friend about them. Every person is different, and it is normal that some tools work for some and not others.

Try a few techniques, and see which ones work for you. Using God's gift of imagination to picture soothing scenes, as well as slowing down your body while repeating compassionate truths, will also help you soothe yourself. These tools can bring you comfort when you are not distressed as well as help bring calm when you are troubled or upset.

As also mentioned in chapter 8, if these exercises are not enough I encourage you to contact a therapist who has been trained in a special kind of therapy called EMDR (Eye Movement Desensitization and Reprocessing; www.emdria.org or www.emdr.com) to help you get unstuck. EMDR is an effective treatment that can help you put distressing life experiences in the past.

Butterfly Hug

The Butterfly Hug is helpful in lots of situations.[1] It can bring comfort when you are upset and is calming and soothing for any reason. Here's what you do: cross your arms over your chest so your right hand touches your left shoulder and your left hand touches your right shoulder. Rest your arms comfortably. Breathe in slowly and completely while you gently and slowly tap the tips of your fingers alternately against your shoulders: left, right, left, right, and so on. This rhythmic motion will often bring soothing feelings and sensations as you comfort yourself.

If desired, add positive statements that bring you comfort. Make them your own for your situation. Perhaps you might say to yourself, *I'll be okay*, or *I'm in God's hands*. Practice this for three to five minutes or until you find yourself becoming more calm and soothed. Some people prefer light tapping on their thighs, which will help bring the same calming effect. If you'd like, write in your journal what it was like to use the Butterfly Hug to calm yourself.

Abdominal Breathing

Abdominal Breathing can be very helpful in slowing down your system and bringing calm. When we breathe deeply all the way into our abdomen, it slows our heart rate, regulates our blood pressure, and helps calm our system.

Here's what you do: close your eyes. Put one hand on your stomach and imagine that there is a balloon inside it. Inhale, and notice how this imaginary balloon grows and pushes your hand up. Exhale, and notice how the balloon deflates. Allow yourself to continue this natural breathing with your hand going up as you breathe in and down as you breathe out. If you become distracted, bring yourself gently back to this exercise. If you'd like, add calming statements that bring you comfort, such as: *I'll be okay. I'm taking in clean, fresh air and exhaling stress.* Make these statements your own. Practice this for three to five minutes, which should be about sixty breaths. Focus on exhaling can calm your brain right down. If you'd like, write in your journal what it was like to use Abdominal Breathing to calm yourself.

Peaceful Place

It can be helpful to create a peaceful, conflict-free place in your mind in order to seek rest. This could be a place you create in your imagination or a real place you've been before. Imagine what it looks like, any sounds and smells, the experience of being there, and so on. Soak that in. You may want to add positive statements that bring you comfort. *I'll be okay. I'm okay right now. I can find solace or rest here.*

As you experience this place, breathe in the peace and comfort of being there as you exhale stress with each breath. Notice how your body responds to being in this place, and allow relaxation and comfort to soothe you. If you'd like, write in your journal what it was like to use the Peaceful Place to calm yourself.

Protective Person

Imagine a protective, nurturing person.[2] This could be Jesus or someone in your life who was or is nurturing to you. It isn't unusual to have trouble imagining a nurturing person. If this is true for you, allow yourself to imagine a mother bear nurturing her cubs, or other animal mothers you have seen care for their offspring. You can also picture a fictional character from a book or movie.

This exercise can be soothing whether you are in the picture yourself or whether you are watching this nurturance and protection being given to another. Whatever you imagine, soak it in. Take some slow, deep breaths, and allow it to permeate you from head to toe. If you'd like, write in your journal what it was like to imagine this Protective Person to calm yourself.

Container Exercise

When you are distressed, you can use the Container Exercise to give yourself some emotional space.[3] Sometimes, if you are feeling really distressed, it can be helpful to create a container in your mind where you can temporarily send your distressing thoughts and feelings for safekeeping. The goal is to get some relief in the moment; later, process them when you have the time, energy, and support from others (such as a therapist or friend). The goal is not to suppress or reject these strong reactions but to get some relief and then choose the best possible time to deal with them.

Here's how you do this. Imagine some sort of secure container in your mind's eye that will be strong enough to hold all the distressing thoughts and feelings you are having. These may include memories, images, thoughts, physical sensations, sounds, smells, or emotions.

Use your creativity to decide what this container looks like. Notice the size, shape, color, texture, what it is made of, and so forth. You will come up with your own creation. Some examples I've heard of include a safe, office drawer, shipping container, crate, dumpster, container for hazardous waste, beautiful box, vase, or glass jar. Realize that this container is strong enough and big enough to hold all your distressing thoughts and feelings. It also needs to have a way to make it safe and secure (such as a lock or a chain holding it closed). In addition, it needs to have a special point of access so that you can send future distressing thoughts and feelings into it without opening the whole container. I imagine an airlock opening that can take distressing thoughts and feelings in but not allow them to come back out.

Now imagine taking your distressing thoughts and feelings and sending them to the container without looking at any of them specifically. Some people imagine a movement of smoke, oil, or mist that moves into the container until as much as can go in there goes in. After you get as much in there as you can think of, shut the door or opening securely and put a lock or seal on it so those distressing thoughts and feelings have a place to stay.

Notice how it feels to have a place for these distressing thoughts and feelings. Notice the little bit of relief, peace, or space that you feel. Tell yourself these thoughts and feelings can stay there for now, until you go back with the help, support, and time you need to address them a little bit at a time.

Next, decide where you want to store this container. Many of my clients leave it in my office, place it at the feet of Jesus, or send it to outer space or the bottom of the sea. You decide where you want it to go and send it there. After you've done this exercise, remember to send any other distressing thoughts and feelings that pop up later into the container through the outside secure entrance. This is a valuable tool to have when you are emotionally triggered or distressed and cannot process your internal reactions at the time.

I hope these ways of interacting with yourself when distressed have been helpful to you. Learning about different ways to soothe yourself when distressed as well as different tools to contain your emotions when needed are all part of a healthy growth process. Here's something you might say to yourself about all you are learning:

It feels good to learn some ways of interacting with myself when I am bothered or distressed. I've learned that these will help me calm myself and treat myself with compassion. It is encouraging to know that I am not supposed to just know how to do this, but that everyone has to learn these skills. I feel a little bit hopeful that I can start to practice the exercises that work for me.

Concluding Reflections

As we come to the close of this chapter, take a moment to check in with yourself about how you are doing. If you would like, ponder the questions below to help process what you've read:

1. What type of self-soothing experiences did you receive growing up? How do you soothe yourself now?

2. What was it like to realize the habits you've employed to reduce your anxiety were ones you happened upon and that healthier skills can be learned?

3. What response did you have to the explanation of the effects of trauma and distressing life events? What kind of new understanding do you have regarding any ongoing struggles you are dealing with?

4. What exercises were the most helpful for you? How did they help?

5. How and when can you practice the exercises that make a difference for you on a regular basis?

10

Closing and Encouragement

We all need a compassionate friend in life. It was not a coincidence that you picked up this book. There is a place in you that has been desiring compassion and understanding. How wonderful that you have taken the steps to learn how to strengthen this relationship with yourself.

A Little Extra Help

Just like anything new, it can be easy to stray from this new way of relating to yourself. With the busyness and demands of life, it probably hasn't become a habit yet . . . but it can! Following are some ideas you can build into your daily life to continue developing the compassionate relationship you have already begun.

1. *Stay self-aware.* Resist the urge to "veg out," live on autopilot, or give up your choices to the demands and urgencies of life. Make a personal commitment to be aware of your thoughts, feelings, needs, and intuition. Check in with

yourself each morning and evening. Ask yourself how you are doing, ask yourself what you need, and remind yourself that you want to be a compassionate friend to yourself.

2. *Make small and meaningful changes in your life.* Realize that even a small change, such as considering *your* needs in a situation, will make a huge difference over time. Notice the things that stood out to you in this book and that had an impact on you personally. It may have been the way you talked to yourself, the self-soothing techniques shared, the biblical basis for self-compassion, understanding your needs and emotions, or one of the many other tools and information shared. Commit to changing one small thing each day and notice the difference it makes.

3. *Practice talking kindly to yourself.* We talk to ourselves all day long. Decide to care for yourself by speaking to yourself with kindness and compassion. If you struggle with this, you are not alone. Most people do. You can listen to recordings of some of these self-compassionate messages by going to www.KimFredrickson.com.

   Notice the way you speak to yourself. Even if you say something negative, you can stop and say to yourself, *No. I am not going to speak to myself this way. I will speak to myself with truth and grace about this situation.* It is fine to go back and correct a misstep.

4. *Ask for what you need.* As you become more aware of yourself and your needs, allow yourself to ask for what you need from yourself, God, and others. Remember, use wisdom in asking those who are available *and* safe. Refer to chapter 6 and decide where you'd like to start on your self-care plan. Ask for help and support as needed. Resist the urge to hint. Ask directly.

5. *Practice being a compassionate emotion coach to yourself.* Review chapter 7 to help build a positive relationship with

yourself by being compassionate with your emotions. Refer to the six steps to come alongside yourself and your emotions in healthy ways.

6. *Schedule times for self-soothing.* Look over chapters 8 and 9 and notice which self-soothing and calming ways of interacting with yourself made a difference for you. Schedule times to practice these skills each day. For some it may be first thing in the morning, for others before bed, and for others perhaps another time. Pay attention to what works for you and take that time for yourself. With repetition, these skills become increasingly automatic.

7. *Encourage and validate yourself.* Try to build in regular times of being your own encourager and validator. Resist the urge to wait for someone else to do this for you. When you step back from the situation at hand, you will be able to find character traits, motives, and actions you can encourage yourself about.

8. *Seek comfort and connection from God.* God loves you and wants a close relationship with you. He is the source of comfort and connection, and he is the author of grace! There is no sin or mistake so big that cannot be forgiven by him. His arms are open wide to you. Find ways to see him in nature and in your world.

9. Check out appendix C, *Quick Start: How to Bounce Back after You've Messed Up.*

In Conclusion

I am proud of you and the steps you took in picking up this book. There is hope as you create that compassionate relationship with yourself. Keep connected to your inner self as you build this new way of relating to yourself a little bit each day. You are valuable, you matter, and you deserve compassion and care!

Verses on God's Love, Care, and Compassion for Us

Reading, praying, and meditating on God's Word is healing and transforming. There are many verses that highlight God's love, care, and value of us, as well as the compassionate ways he sees and relates to us. You may note that *compassion* is often translated as *mercy* in the Bible. Mulling over a verse each morning and evening will bring the healing truth of God's love and compassion for you deep in your heart and soul.

God's Love

For I am the LORD your God
who takes hold of your right hand
and says to you, Do not fear;
I will help you. (Isa. 41:13)

The LORD appeared to us in the past, saying:
I have loved you with an everlasting love;
I have drawn you with unfailing kindness. (Jer. 31:3)

Can a mother forget the baby at her breast
and have no compassion on the child she has borne?
Though she may forget,
I will not forget you! (Isa. 49:15)

See what great love the Father has lavished on us, that we should be called children of God! And that is what we are! The reason the world does not know us is that it did not know him. (1 John 3:1)

But the LORD said to Samuel, "Do not consider his appearance or his height, for I have rejected him. The LORD does not look at the things people look at. People look at the outward appearance, but the LORD looks at the heart." (1 Sam. 16:7)

"For I know the plans I have for you," declares the LORD, "plans to prosper you and not to harm you, plans to give you hope and a future." (Jer. 29:11)

The LORD your God is with you,
the Mighty Warrior who saves.
He will take great delight in you;
in his love he will no longer rebuke you,
but will rejoice over you with singing. (Zeph. 3:17)

For God so loved the world that he gave his one and only Son, that whoever believes in him shall not perish but have eternal life. For God did not send his Son into the world to condemn the world, but to save the world through him. (John 3:16–17)

Give thanks to the LORD, for he is good.
His love endures forever.
Give thanks to the God of gods.
His love endures forever.
Give thanks to the Lord of lords:
His love endures forever. (Ps. 136:1–3)

[I pray] that Christ may dwell in your hearts through faith. And I pray that you, being rooted and established in love, may have power, together with all the Lord's holy people, to grasp how wide and long and high and deep is the love of Christ, and to know this love that surpasses knowledge—that you may be filled to the measure of all the fullness of God. (Eph. 3:17–19)

> Your love, Lord, reaches to the heavens,
>   your faithfulness to the skies.
> Your righteousness is like the highest mountains,
>   your justice like the great deep.
> You, Lord, preserve both people and animals.
> How priceless is your unfailing love, O God!
>   People take refuge in the shadow of your wings.
>   (Ps. 36:5–7)

The word of the Lord came to me, saying,
    "Before I formed you in the womb I knew you,
    before you were born I set you apart." (Jer. 1:4–5)

This is how God showed his love among us: He sent his one and only Son into the world that we might live through him. This is love: not that we loved God, but that he loved us and sent his Son as an atoning sacrifice for our sins. (1 John 4:9–10)

> "Though the mountains be shaken
>   and the hills be removed,
> yet my unfailing love for you will not be shaken
>   nor my covenant of peace be removed,"
>   says the Lord, who has compassion on you.
>   (Isa. 54:10)

For this is what the high and exalted One says—
    he who lives forever, whose name is holy:
"I live in a high and holy place,
    but also with the one who is contrite and lowly in
        spirit,
to revive the spirit of the lowly
    and to revive the heart of the contrite." (Isa. 57:15)

For you created my inmost being;
   you knit me together in my mother's womb.
I praise you because I am fearfully and wonderfully made;
   your works are wonderful,
   I know that full well.
My frame was not hidden from you
   when I was made in the secret place,
   when I was woven together in the depths of the earth.
Your eyes saw my unformed body;
   all the days ordained for me were written in your book
   before one of them came to be. (Ps. 139:13–16)

Yet to all who did receive him, to those who believed in his name, he gave the right to become children of God. (John 1:12)

Are not five sparrows sold for two pennies? Yet not one of them is forgotten by God. Indeed, the very hairs of your head are all numbered. Don't be afraid; you are worth more than many sparrows. (Luke 12:6–7)

Come to me, all you who are weary and burdened, and I will give you rest. Take my yoke upon you and learn from me, for I am gentle and humble in heart, and you will find rest for your souls. For my yoke is easy and my burden is light. (Matt. 11:28–30)

Though my father and mother forsake me,
   the LORD will receive me. (Ps. 27:10)

Know that the LORD is God.
   It is he who made us, and we are his;
   we are his people, the sheep of his pasture. (Ps. 100:3)

But now, this is what the LORD says—
   he who created you, Jacob,
   he who formed you, Israel:
"Do not fear, for I have redeemed you;
   I have summoned you by name; you are mine."
   (Isa. 43:1)

The LORD is with me; I will not be afraid.
What can mere mortals do to me? (Ps. 118:6)

No one will be able to stand against you all the days of your life.
As I was with Moses, so I will be with you; I will never leave you
nor forsake you. (Josh. 1:5)

> Surely your goodness and love will follow me
>   all the days of my life,
> and I will dwell in the house of the LORD
>   forever. (Ps. 23:6)

> Give thanks to the LORD, for he is good;
>   his love endures forever. (1 Chron. 16:34)

> But I am like an olive tree
>   flourishing in the house of God;
> I trust in God's unfailing love
>   for ever and ever. (Ps. 52:8)

God's Compassion

> Yet he was merciful;
>   he forgave their iniquities
>   and did not destroy them.
> Time after time he restrained his anger
>   and did not stir up his full wrath.
> He remembered that they were but flesh,
>   a passing breeze that does not return.
>   (Ps. 78:38–39)

> He heals the brokenhearted
>   and binds up their wounds. (Ps. 147:3)

Grace and peace to you from God our Father and the Lord Jesus
Christ. Praise be to the God and Father of our Lord Jesus Christ,
the Father of compassion and the God of all comfort, who comforts

us in all our troubles, so that we can comfort those in any trouble
with the comfort we ourselves receive from God. (2 Cor. 1:2–4)

When he saw the crowds, he had compassion on them, because
they were harassed and helpless, like sheep without a shepherd.
(Matt. 9:36)

> But you, Lord, are a compassionate and gracious God,
>   slow to anger, abounding in love and faithfulness.
>   (Ps. 86:15)

This is what the LORD Almighty said: "Administer true justice;
show mercy and compassion to one another. Do not oppress
the widow or the fatherless, the foreigner or the poor. Do not
plot evil against each other." (Zech. 7:9–10)

> You, Lord, are forgiving and good,
>   abounding in love to all who call to you. (Ps. 86:5)

> The LORD is compassionate and gracious,
>   slow to anger, abounding in love. (Ps. 103:8)

Praise be to the God and Father of our Lord Jesus Christ! In his
great mercy he has given us new birth into a living hope through
the resurrection of Jesus Christ from the dead. (1 Pet. 1:3)

> Who is a God like you,
>   who pardons sin and forgives the transgression
>   of the remnant of his inheritance?
> You do not stay angry forever
>   but delight to show mercy. (Mic. 7:18)

> Shout for joy, you heavens;
>   rejoice, you earth;
>   burst into song, you mountains!
> For the LORD comforts his people
>   and will have compassion on his afflicted ones.
>   (Isa. 49:13)

Have mercy on me, O God,
   according to your unfailing love;
according to your great compassion
   blot out my transgressions. (Ps. 51:1)

Because of the LORD's great love we are not consumed,
   for his compassions never fail.
They are new every morning;
   great is your faithfulness.
I say to myself, "The LORD is my portion;
   therefore I will wait for him."
The LORD is good to those whose hope is in him,
   to the one who seeks him. (Lam. 3:22–25)

Appendix B

Using This Material
with Groups

I've had many groups use this material, and here are some ideas
to keep your group safe as you process this material together.
Thanks so much to those of you who have shared your input
with me in this regard.

The most important part of a group is emotional safety and
trust. Begin by establishing some basic group rules that everyone
agrees to follow. Some of these may include:

Confidentiality is to be maintained completely. Nothing that
is brought up in the group should leave the group. Names,
situations, and anecdotes should not be shared with anyone
who is not a part of the group.

Be consistent and on time. This establishes trust and helps
everyone to feel a part of the group.

No shoulds, oughts, musts, or advice. Group members are
most helped when listened to, shown understanding, and

empathized with. Shoulds, oughts, musts, and advice-giving are not helpful.

Participate, but don't dominate. One of the most healing aspects of being in a group is the opportunity to be real and share what is really going on in our lives. To do this, each member needs to allow everyone time to share.

Allow feelings. It is common to want to jump in to "rescue" or help someone who is feeling deeply. Sometimes another's tears, fears, or deep sorrow may be uncomfortable for us, and we might feel tempted to offer comfort too quickly. What is most helpful in those situations is allowing the person to share and then validating their feelings with understanding and compassion.

If you feel hurt or misunderstood, please try to share this within your group or privately with your leader. Part of growth involves working through tough spots rather than just leaving.

Having these group rules will keep the group safe and build trust as you share personal information with one another.

Helpful Tips for Processing as a Group

- Don't be in a hurry to get through the material. Let your need guide how fast you process it.
- Each member should read the chapter ahead of time and make notes about their own personal response to what has been shared.
- When you meet together, take turns reading a paragraph at a time and then share your responses together.
- When you get to the self-compassion statements, read them out loud together and discuss how they impacted you.

- If you want, have each group member bring in a picture of themselves when they were little. This will give you compassion for yourself when you were small and will increase compassion for other group members as well. Use your picture as a bookmark and frequently look at yourself as a little one . . . sweet, precious, and lovable. Having compassion for the little you in that picture can begin to build a more compassionate response to your adult self.

- End every group session with each member's plan to be self-compassionate that week.

Quick Start:
How to Bounce Back after
You've Messed Up

Yes, it's bound to happen. You're human and you mess up, just like me. Here is a succinct way to help you bounce back after you've messed up, didn't know something, couldn't predict the future, and so on. You may want to copy these pages for multiple uses or process your thoughts and feelings in a journal.

Basic Truths to Remember

- You're human. You're supposed to mess up. That's how you learn. You can't change your tendency to sin, goof up, not know everything, and so on.
- What you can change is your response to your mistakes.
- God already knows what happened, and wants to help you. He's already paid the price for our sins. You have

the chance to turn toward him and accept his mercy, love, and compassion.

- You can change how you respond to yourself, God, and others, and you can use what has happened for growth.
- You can approach yourself with grace and truth as a compassionate friend rather than as a critic.

So, let's get started . . .

1. Figure out what happened.
Sometimes when it feels like we messed up it is really obvious where we went wrong. Other times we may assume we messed up but actually didn't, and other times something hard did happen but it had nothing to do with us.

List the situation:

_____

_____

_____

_____

What do you wish you had done differently? Was this even a possibility, given what you knew and the situation at hand?

_____

_____

_____

_____

A. If you did do something wrong, ask yourself these questions:

Did I do what I did on purpose?

_____

Am I truly sorry?

_____

If my friend did the same thing to someone else, would they deserve to be forgiven? What would I say to them?

_____

_____

Do I really think I can go through life without making major mistakes and hurting others—even those I love?

_____

What fears or concerns did I have that caused me to say or do what I now regret?

_____

_____

Knowing what I know now, what would I do differently?

_____

_____

_____

As you read the above list of questions, don't use this list to shame yourself. Use these questions to help you understand yourself and be compassionate to yourself. Let yourself know that, *Yes I made a mistake. I am of worth and value, and will address this mistake directly.*

B. If you didn't actually do anything wrong, notice that it is normal to feel regret that something happened without being responsible for it. Tell yourself the truth:

- *I feel bad about what happened and realize I'm not responsible for what happened.*
- *It is normal for me to feel regret that things turned out the way they did, because I am a caring person.*
- *I will pray for this situation and people involved if I choose to and will ask God to take care of those involved, including myself.*

C. If you're not sure, ask yourself if there is a way that, unintentionally, you may have contributed to what happened. Be kind to yourself as you look at this. The intention is to see if you had a part in what went wrong in order to repair and learn from this situation.

- *Is there a way I may have contributed to this problem?*
- *If someone else is telling me I messed up, is there any truth in what is being shared with me?*
- *What would others in this situation say to themselves?*
- *What other possible conclusions could be made in this situation?*
- *What would the kindest person I know say to me about this situation?*

2. Approach yourself with kindness, compassion, and understanding with what you've discovered.

A. Talk to yourself with compassion. Decide to approach yourself with grace and truth in this moment. Use the "on the one hand, on the other hand" tool shared in chapter 4.

- On the one hand (whatever the negative is)

_____

and

- On the other hand (compassion and understanding for self)

_____

_____

Write yourself a caring and compassionate message about what you are going through, even if you had a part in the problem. Be sure to include a balanced understanding of what went on, rather than a black-and-white viewpoint (see chapter 8 for more ideas).

_____

_____

_____

_____

Encourage yourself that even though something regrettable has happened, you can still be kind to yourself and the other person. Let yourself know that you can feel regret and learn from what happened, and can take the steps necessary to repair the hurt, if appropriate.

B. Get the support you need. What kind of support can you raise for yourself in this moment? Ask yourself some important questions:

- *What do I need right now?* (See chapter 6 for more ideas.)
- *Do I need help with physical needs such as sleep, rest, food, water, or exercise?*
- *Do I need spiritual support and connection from God right now?*
- *Do I need emotional support? Do I feel alone in this? Who is a kind and truthful person I could run this scenario by?*
- *What is one way to get the support I need right now?*
- *What are compassionate words I'd like to hear from myself?*
- *Would it help to journal, pray, cry, or take a run?*

C. Practice self-soothing and calming techniques.

- *What are some things I've done in the past that bring me comfort?*
- *What type of soothing words do I need to hear from myself right now?*
- *Are there Scriptures or music that would be comforting to me?*
- *Are there self-soothing exercises in chapter 9 that could help me right now?*

3. What do you need to do for yourself emotionally?
It is very common to do or say things we regret when we are emotionally upset. Part of bouncing back from messing up, or from tough experiences, involves working with your emotions in healthy ways (see chapter 7). As you look back on what happened for the purpose of learning, ask yourself some important questions:

- *When did I start feeling distressed?*
- *What were the warning signs that things were not okay?*
- *What did I need?*
- *How could I have taken a break to calm myself down?*
- *What could I have done to address the problem without doing something I later regretted?*
- *What compassionate statements could I have said to myself?*
- *What will I do next time when emotionally upset to both comfort myself and to not do or say something I later regret?*

4. If another person was involved, is there anything you need to do to make things right?

As you ask yourself the following questions, don't use this list to shame yourself. Use it to help you understand yourself and see if there are any steps you'd like to take to make things right regarding the situation you are thinking of.

- *What is my understanding of how the other person was hurt?*
- *Do I truly understand how the other person was feeling?*
- *Have I apologized and asked forgiveness from the person I hurt?*
- *What do I specifically need to apologize for?*
- *If I feel a nudge to take some action to make things right, what do I need in order to take the next step?*

5. What have you learned from this Quick Start exercise?

This may be the first time you found a way to step back from a difficult experience and come alongside yourself as a compassionate friend to figure it out. Notice what it is like to approach yourself with grace and truth and with the goal of understanding what happened, what you need, and what to do about it.

- *What have I learned about myself?*
- *What have I learned about the other person?*
- *What have I learned about what I need to change in my life to lower the chances of this happening again (more sleep, less busyness, more self-care, waiting to react, paying attention to the warning signs)?*
- *What have I learned about how to treat myself with grace and truth when I mess up?*

Some Final Words of Encouragement

It is normal to mess up. It is impossible not to. The greatest outcome when we mess up is to draw near to ourselves as a compassionate friend as we learn from our mistakes. Make it your goal to be both compassionate and truthful with yourself while addressing what happened directly. Turn to God for strength and wisdom. Treat yourself kindly and get the kind of support you need. Be brave and try to right a wrong you caused, even if it was unintentional. You can recover. You can work through each situation, grow from it, and let the pain go.

Notes

Chapter 1 Why Self-Compassion Is So Important

1. Kristin Neff, *Self-Compassion* (New York: HarperCollins, 2011), 123, 170.
2. Ibid., 165–66.
3. Ibid., 110.

Chapter 2 A Look Inside

1. Gary Lundberg and Joy Lundberg, *I Don't Have to Make Everything All Better* (New York: Penguin Books, 2000), 4, 6.
2. The term "good-enough parent" was coined by British psychoanalyst D. W. Winnicott. He conceded that parenting was difficult and complex, and that no one could be a perfect parent. Because of children's resilience, most parents could be "good enough" to help their children make a good start. See D. W. Winnicott, "The Maturational Processes and the Facilitating Environment," to learn more.

Chapter 3 Why It Is So Hard to Be Compassionate with Ourselves

1. Henry Cloud et al., *Secrets of Your Family Tree* (Chicago: Moody, 1995), 148.
2. Adapted from Tim Clinton and Gary Sibcy, *Attachments* (Franklin, TN: Integrity, 2002), 49–144.

Chapter 5 How Self-Compassion Helps All of Our Relationships

1. Neff, *Self-Compassion*, 110.

Chapter 7 Be Compassionate with Your Emotions

1. John Gottman and Joan Declaire, *Raising an Emotionally Intelligent Child* (New York: Simon & Schuster, 1997), 42–68.
2. Ibid., 69–137.

Chapter 8 Practical Tools to Build a Compassionate Relationship with Yourself

1. Personal conversation with David K. Fredrickson, ThM, PhD, June 1, 2012. The general stewardship rule is to avoid all damage to self if possible (for example, run away from persecution if possible, and don't volunteer for mistreatment). There are exceptions, but these are carefully highlighted in Scripture as the unique life calling for some and are the exception, not the rule. These special life callings rarely involve giving up boundaries and good stewardship of one's life outside of physical safety. In these special cases, the person is called to give up boundary maintenance specifically and only with others who don't know any better and/or can't be stopped. An example of this is Paul regularly submitting to stonings and beatings from angry nonbelievers (Acts 16:15; 14:17). Yet, with the Corinthians (believers) he demanded they respect his authority, his rules, and him as a person (2 Cor. 13:1–6). With Peter, he demanded that Peter respect and follow Paul's example regarding eating with Gentiles (Gal. 2:11–14).

2. Thanks to Rick Hanson, PhD (www.RickHanson.net), for this tool, presented at a workshop in Sacramento, *Taking in the Good*, November 2009.

Chapter 9 Practice Self-Soothing Techniques

1. This exercise based on "The Butterfly Hug," originally developed by Lucy Artigas and Ignacio Jarero. For more information see Ignacio Jarero, Lucina Artigas, and John Hartung, "EMDR Integrative Group Treatment Protocol: A Postdisaster Trauma Intervention for Children and Adults," *Traumatology* 12, no. 2 (2006): 121–29, doi: 10.1177/1534765606294561.

2. This exercise based on information shared by Philip Manfield, *Dyadic Resourcing: Creating a Foundation for Processing Trauma* (CreateSpace Independent Publishing Platform, 2010), 67–93.

3. This exercise based on information shared by Katy Murray, "Container," *Journal of EMDR Practice and Research* 5, no. 1 (2011): 29–32, doi: http://dx.doi.org/10.1891/1933-3196.5.1.29.

Bibliography

Carder, Dave, Earl Henslin, John Townsend, Henry Cloud, and Alice Brawand. *Secrets of Your Family Tree: Healing for Adult Children of Dysfunctional Families.* Chicago: Moody, 1995.

Clinton, Tim, and Gary Sibcy. *Attachments: Why You Love, Feel, and Act the Way You Do.* Franklin, TN: Integrity, 2002.

Clinton, Tim, and Joshua Straub. *God Attachment: Why You Believe, Act and Feel the Way You Do About God.* New York: Howard Books, 2010.

Cloud, Henry, and John Townsend. *Boundaries: When to Say Yes, How to Say No to Take Control of Your Life.* Grand Rapids: Zondervan, 1992.

———. *Boundaries in Marriage.* Grand Rapids: Zondervan, 1999.

———. *How to Have That Difficult Conversation You've Been Avoiding: With Your Spouse, Adult Child, Boss, Coworker, Best Friend, Parent, or Someone You're Dating.* Grand Rapids: Zondervan, 2005.

Gilbert, Paul. *The Compassionate Mind: A New Approach to Life's Challenges.* Oakland, CA: New Harbinger, 2010.

Gottman, John. *What Am I Feeling?* Seattle, WA: Parenting Press, 2004.

Gottman, John, and Joan Declaire. *Raising an Emotionally Intelligent Child: The Heart of Parenting.* New York: Simon & Schuster, 1998.

Jarero, Ignacio, Lucina Artigas, and J. Hartung. "EMDR Integrative Group Treatment Protocol: A Postdisaster Intervention for Children and Adults." *Traumatology* 12, no. 2 (2006): 121–29. doi: 10.1177/1534765606294561.

Lundberg, Gary, and Joy Lundberg. *I Don't Have to Make Everything All Better.* New York: Penguin Books, 2000.

Manfield, Philip. *Dyadic Resourcing: Creating a Foundation for Processing Trauma.* CreateSpace Independent Publishing Platform, 2010.

Seubert, Andrew. *The Courage to Feel: A Practical Guide to the Power and Freedom of Emotional Honesty.* West Conshohocken, PA: Infinity, 2008.

Shapiro, Francine. *Getting Past Your Past: Take Control of Your Life with Self-Help Techniques from EMDR.* New York: Rodale Books, 2012.

Stoop, David, and David Mastellar. *Forgiving Our Parents, Forgiving Ourselves: Healing Adult Children of Dysfunctional Families.* Ventura, CA: Regal, 2011.

Townsend, John. *Beyond Boundaries: Learning to Trust Again in Relationships.* Grand Rapids: Zondervan, 2011.

Welford, Mary. *The Power of Self-Compassion: Using Compassion-Focused Therapy to End Self-Criticism and Build Self-Confidence.* Oakland, CA: New Harbinger, 2013.

Winnicott, D. W. "The Maturational Processes and the Facilitating Environment: Studies in the Theory of Emotional Development." Edited by M. Masud R. Khan. *The International Psycho-Analytical Library,* 64 (1965):1–276. http://www.abebe.org.br/wp-content/uploads/Donald-Winnicott-The-Maturational-Process-and-the-Facilitating-Environment-Studies-in-the-Theory-of-Emotional-Development-1965.pdf.

Resources

This book includes many self-compassionate statements to say to yourself as well as helpful exercises to practice. Many people notice that these comforting messages sink in at a deeper level when listened to. These are available for purchase as a CD or as a downloadable mp3 recording read by Kim. Go to http://www.cdbaby.com/kimfredrickson to purchase these recordings as a CD, or go to www.amazon.com or iTunes (search under "Kim Fredrickson") to download as an mp3.

Digital mp3 recordings and accompanying handouts on each of the topics below are also available. Visit http://www.gumroad.com/kimfredrickson for more information and to purchase and download.

Building Emotional Closeness in Your Relationships
Listen in to gain understanding and skills to help you build emotional closeness in all of your relationships. Without emotional closeness people feel disconnected and misunderstood, and have a hard time recovering from conflicts.

Improving Your Relationships with Validation and Empathy
Listen and learn how the simple but powerful tools of validation and empathy will help all your relationships. By learning how

to help or influence others without "taking over" or trying to "fix" them, we provide caring and direction without taking on misplaced responsibility and guilt. These tools will help every relationship in your life.

Healthy Communication Skills

Listen and learn practical communication skills to express yourself effectively and clearly, as well as learn strategies to handle those who might derail you. Won't it feel good to express both your thoughts and feelings clearly? This recording includes two dynamic role plays demonstrating these skills and worksheets to help you express yourself.

Learning How to Deal with Your Emotions

Most of us are scared of, disconnected from, and/or controlled by our feelings. We will come together to learn about and work with our feelings, and learn a four-step process that will transform our stumbling, discomfort, and disconnection with our feelings into emotional growth and health. We will also learn skills to keep ourselves emotionally grounded. Becoming more emotionally competent will benefit all our relationships.

Skills for Talking through Hard Topics

It is normal to shy away from or avoid talking about hard topics. Learn effective ways to turn toward and work through difficult topics. Learn rules for "fighting fair" as well as how to repair hurts and communication in relationships. This recording also looks at how men and women approach and process talking about hard topics differently, and includes a role play.

Kim Fredrickson, MS, has been a licensed marriage and family therapist for thirty years and is a certified Christian life coach.

Kim is a sought-after speaker on the topics of parenting, building healthy relationships, self-care, and self-compassion. Kim loves helping people become equipped spiritually, emotionally, and intellectually with practical skills to live more effective and fulfilling lives.

She and Dave have been married for thirty-seven years and have two wonderful adult children. In her spare time, Kim enjoys gardening, reading, scrapbooking, and spending time with family and friends. During the writing of this book Kim encountered extra opportunities to be compassionate with herself. She completed successful treatment for breast cancer in March 2014, and four days later started a battle with a progressive lung disease that developed as a result of the chemotherapy and radiation. Kim lives out these principles on a daily basis and would appreciate your prayers.

For practical, encouraging help with your relationships and personal growth, check out Kim's website: www.KimFredrickson.com. There you will find free articles to help with your relationships, as well as free encouraging audio recordings and recordings of her recent workshops.